Markers VI

Journal of the Association for Gravestone Studies

Edited by
Theodore Chase

UNIVERSITY
PRESS OF
AMERICA

LANHAM • NEW YORK • LONDON

Copyright © 1989 by

University Press of America,® Inc.

4720 Boston Way
Lanham, MD 20706

3 Henrietta Street
London WC2E 8LU England

All rights reserved

Printed in the United States of America

British Cataloging in Publication Information Available

Co-published by arrangement with
the Association for Gravestone Studies

"Afro-American Gravemarkers in North Carolina"
© 1989 by M. Ruth Little

ISBN (Perfect): 0-8191-7317-7 (pbk. alk. paper)
ISBN (Cloth): 0-8191-7316-9 (alk. paper)
LCN: 81-642903

All University Press of America books are produced on acid-free paper.
The paper used in this publication meets the minimum requirements of American
National Standard for Information Sciences—Permanence of Paper for Printed Library
Materials, ANSI Z39.48–1984.

ASSOCIATION FOR GRAVESTONE STUDIES
EDITORIAL BOARD

Theodore Chase, Editor
David Watters, Associate Editor

John L. Brooke	James A. Slater
Jessie Lie Farber	Richard F. Welch

The editor again wishes to thank the members of the editorial board for their advice and help in the selection and editing of articles for this edition of the journal and to thank Carol Davidson for her continuing assistance in the preparation of copy and layout. We are also grateful to the University of New Hampshire which, through the intervention of David Watters, provided a subsidy for publication of Markers V and generously provided secretarial services in connection with this issue. And finally the editor wishes to credit Daniel and Jessie Lie Farber for the photographs used to illustrate the article entitled "Tributes in Stone and Lapidary Lapses" by Angelika Krüger-Kahloula and the review by Peter Benes of James Slater's book.

Information about the submission of manuscripts for Markers may be obtained from the editor, Theodore Chase, 74 Farm Street, Dover, Massachusetts 02030. For information about other Association for Gravestone Studies publications, membership and activities, write to the executive director, Rosalee Oakley, 46 Plymouth Road, Needham, Massachusetts 02192.

Articles appearing in this journal are annotated and indexed in *Historical Abstracts* and *America: History and Life*.

TABLE OF CONTENTS

	Page
The John Dwight Workshop in Shirley, Massachusetts, 1770-1816 Eloise Sibley West	1
Tributes in Stone and Lapidary Lapses: Commemorating Black People in Eighteenth- and Nineteenth-Century America Angelika Krüger-Kahloula	33
Afro-American Gravemarkers in North Carolina M. Ruth Little	103
Communities of the Dead: Tombstones as a Reflection of Social Organization Paula J. Fenza	137
Camposantos: Sacred Places of the Southwest Laura Sue Sanborn	159
United Above Though Parted Below: The Hand as Symbol on Nineteenth-Century Southwest Ontario Gravestones Nancy-Lou Patterson	181
An Early Christian Athlete: The Epitaph of Aurelius Eutychus of Eumeneia Scott T. Carroll	209
Book Review: *The Colonial Burying Grounds of Eastern Connecticut and The Men Who Made Them*, by James A. Slater Peter Benes	233
Contributors	241
Index	243

Fig. 1   William Simonds, 1758, Shirley.

THE JOHN DWIGHT WORKSHOP
IN SHIRLEY, MASSACHUSETTS, 1770-1816

Eloise Sibley West

Burying grounds throughout central Massachusetts and in areas north and south of Boston contain many gravestones from the workshop of John Dwight in Shirley which are very similar. These stones were described by Harriette Forbes, who wrote: "Having seen a few John Dwights, we can imagine all the others."[1] A recent search has revealed, however, that John Dwight and his son Francis were more versatile than Mrs. Forbes believed. The work of the shop spanned a period of more than fifty years and ended abruptly and tragically in 1816.

John Dwight had two sons who were stonecarvers, a daughter who married a stonecarver, and a grandson who was a stonecarver. Documents pertaining to the Dwight workshop recently discovered in Shirley provide much information about the work of the shop under son Francis and cast new light on the business of gravestone carving in the early 1800s.

John Dwight, stonecarver, was born in Boston about 1740. His father, Captain John Dwight, was lost in a shipwreck in 1744, leaving his only son fatherless at the age of four. His mother's maiden name was said to be Foster.[2]

John's life, before his arrival in Shirley, has not been documented. It can be inferred from a study of the style and distribution of his stones that John spent some time at the workshop of the Foster family in Dorchester, Massachusetts. The Old North Burying Ground there includes stones carved in the Foster style but made by Dwight. A few in the Dorchester cemetery, also by Dwight, are made from the tan-colored, fine-grained stone used by the Fosters. Although he moved to Shirley before the death of the carver James Foster III in 1771, John retained ties with the families living in Dorchester, and carved their gravestones in his Shirley workshop. One can even speculate that John's mother was a Dorchester Foster, but support for this suggestion has not been found.

Little has been written about the life of John Dwight, so probate, town and military records are the only official records available. He came to Shirley as a young man "in good pecuniary circumstances,"[3] skilled in gravestone carving and with experience in farming. John carved stones, chose a wife and bought a farm.

Susanna (Harris) Moors was the widow of Jonathan Moors, who died July 18, 1765. She was Moors's second wife. After their short marriage she was left with only one living child, Abel Moors, born posthumously on January 22, 1766.[4] A daughter was also born to Susanna: "Moors, Eunice, d. Susannah, wid., bp. Apr. 16, 1769."[5] Her birth is not recorded nor is the name of her father. In the records of the Town Clerk of Shirley: "There is a marriage intended between Mr. John Dwight and Mrs. Susanna Moors both of this district." No date of intention or of the marriage is included.[6] John and Susanna were married some time before 1770. All of this suggests, but does not prove, that Eunice was an illegitimate child. John did not adopt her, so perhaps she was not his child.

In 1770 John bought a farm on the banks of Mulpus Brook from the owners, Francis Harris (John's father-in-law) and John Ivory. The house was well known as the site of the first official Town Meeting, in 1753, when Shirley separated from its mother town, Groton.[7] John and Susanna had a busy life tending the farm, filling orders for gravestones and bringing up an ever-increasing family. They had eight children: five girls and three boys, of whom more will be said later.

The founding of a new nation took precious time from personal concerns. John Dwight joined the able-bodied men of Shirley as a private in Henry Haskell's Company of Minute Men, marching to Cambridge after the battle of Lexington. He returned home April 30, 1775, having served thirteen days including marching time, and was paid L1.4.9. He was called again to service at White Plains, New York, in October 1776. There he received a wound in the head that impaired his hearing for life.[8]

John shared responsibilities as a resident of Shirley. The Town "Made choyse of Mr. John Dwight as constable."[9] At the Town Meeting on March 1, 1773, John Dwight was appointed a field driver.[10] When the Reverend Phinehas Whitney accepted the unanimous call of First Parish Church, part of the terms of his "settlement" included twenty cords of wood, to be carried to his door annually. The Town Meeting of March 14, 1777, "Gave John Dwight an order on Jonas Longley Treasurer for getting the Rev. Mr. Whitney wood."[11]

The quarries at Harvard and Lancaster were bustling with business when John opened his workshop. Harvard's Pin Hill quarry seems to be a source of the fine slate that distinguishes his work. Workmen detached slabs from the quarry walls by splitting with wedges. Later it was sawed. Stonecarvers purchased "rights" in a quarry, allowing them to take stone from a certain area. The carvers paid for the stone, per foot, and also for quarry rent. Rights could be sold, divided or used to pay bills owed to other carvers. The inventory in the probate file of Daniel Hastings, a Newton, Massachusetts, stonecutter, includes: "one note signed by John Dwight to be paid in stone at the quarry in Harvard, 25.00." The inventory in the Dwight estate lists: "a right in stone quarry in Harvard ----- 30 dollars."[12]

Dwight chose the dark blue slate of the Pin Hill quarry and soaked it in Mulpus Brook to prepare it for carving. His gravestones, 1 1/4 to 1 3/4 inches thick, look delicate but are surprisingly sturdy. The elaborate stones are four to five feet tall and correspondingly thicker. The back of a Dwight stone has a vertical, grainy texture, resembling tree bark or crepe paper. This is a definite clue to our carver. The flat back is gray, often weathered to rust, and makes the stones easy to identify. The Park family of Groton also used this stone for a few years, but the carving on the face of the stone readily distinguishes the carvers. The Dwight stones have no chisel marks on the back, indicating that the stone must have been split, saving time and heavy work.

The John Dwight gravestones are shaped with a central, curved tympanum and with lower, rounded shoulders that top the narrow side borders. Three-quarters of the stones in this study have this shape. Different patterns are used in the tympanum. Variety has also been achieved by changing the borders and varying the shape of the tablet. There are exceptions in size and shape for special stones. From the late 1790s until 1816, the usual shape of the Dwight stone changed to a high tympanum with short, straight shoulders (Fig. 18). These were used while Francis was carving and are typical of the urn-and-willow period.

The change in gravestone styles did not take place in strict order by date, and the date on the stone is not proof that it was actually carved that year. Buyers chose what they liked. Some preferred the older styles, or bought the simple rather than the more expensive. Some of the stones, obviously back-dated, could have been late orders or replacements. There are stones in Middlesex and Worcester counties that were carved by John Dwight and dated as early as 1764. A few may be back-dated but most have patterns appropriate for the period. This means that John must have had access to the quarry and begun his professional carving before he married and acquired a permanent home.

The earliest stone I have found that can be attributed to John Dwight is that of William Simonds (1758) in the Shirley Center Burial Ground (Fig. 1). It is probably back-dated by several years since it displays the skill of an experienced carver. This stone is not documented but does have many of the elements typical of Dwight's early patterns. The Simonds stone has a round skull with narrow chin, round eyes, pointed nose and visible teeth. The high wings begin at the side of the face, along with the palm fronds.

Hollowed lobes droop from the top. The outside feathers of the wings are ribbed -- a good element for identifying Dwight's work. Pinwheel and teardrop finials (see Figs. 1 and 3) were chosen often. The scroll and leaf border and the lettering are typical of the carver's work. His peculiar mark is barely visible in the corners of the stone's tablet.

This small mark -- an almond-shaped gouge placed diagonally in the corners of the tablet -- is a decisive indicator of Dwight's work and appears on about sixty percent of his stones which have a skull and wings in the tympanum. A close-up shows the position and the comparative size (Fig. 2). Others can be detected in photographs of entire stones (Figs. 1, 3, 5, 6, 7). The mark varies in actual size, is deeply grooved and not conspicuous. Children's stones with plain borders were seldom marked. I have not seen this exact identification used by any other carver.

Fig. 2 John Dwight's mark.

Fig. 3 Patty Pierce, 1780, Fitchburg.

Another type of John Dwight's carving style appears with the bald head, bushy eyebrows and long nose considered appropriate for young Patty Pierce (Fig. 3). The crescent mouth is smiling. The unusual segmented wings were used by Dwight only in this type. The tablet has his mark. Dwight's stones for children were smaller but well carved. This one is about fifteen inches high.

I have used the word "type" to indicate a group of stones with similar face and wings in the tympanum and similar side borders. When the face and wings change, a new type is emerging. Abraham Wheeler's stone represents the type most frequently carved by John Dwight and is of the type referred to by Mrs. Forbes (Fig. 4). The face in the tympanum is longer, more mature than that in Patty's stone (Fig. 3). The head has rope-like hair (or wig), the chin is long and narrow and the mouth small. The wide-spreading wings have outside feathers that are ribbed. These single, ribbed feathers are another indication of Dwight's work, even in his later types. Most of this group have the peculiar Dwight marks.

Teardrops are an essential part of Dwight's designs. He used them, in some form, from 1764 until he stopped carving. They made a single border surrounding the tympanum or a double border (Figs. 4 and 9), outlined parts of the tablet (Fig. 12) or completely surrounded the stone (Fig. 16). In groups of three, they sometimes appeared in the finials (Figs. 4 and 5). And they were used to form lobes in the border panels. In the Wheeler stone (Fig. 4) the center of the lobe has been carved longer and pointed. The side border of this stone alternates lobes with leafed scrolls, one of the four patterns used with this type.

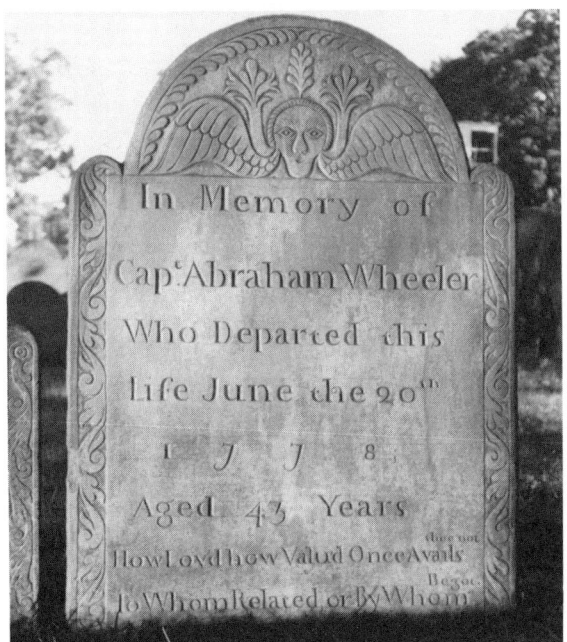

Fig. 4 Capt. Abraham Wheeler, 1778, Dorchester.

Fig. 5   Lieut. Hezekiah Sawtell, 1779, Groton.

Fig. 6   Martha Metchel, 1782, Lunenberg

In 1779 John Dwight carved a stone nearly five feet tall, with an unusual shape, for "A Beloved Friend." It is one of the best of his carvings in this period (Fig. 5). This stone for Hezekiah Sawtell (1779) has a tympanum border of berries and side borders with a lovely combination of scrolls and flowers. The bottom border is simpler -- a usual practice among carvers.

Letters and numbers on the tablet are also an aid in determining the identity of a carver. The stone of Martha Metchel shows this clearly (Fig. 6). Characteristic letters are: a tiny, short 't', smaller than the other letters; a 'y' that curls upward toward the line; and the wedge-shaped cross bars on 't' and 'f'. The 'M' is deeply cut on the right side. The letters 'h' and 'l' have serifs resembling handles. Numbers 1, 2, 8, 0 are very small, while 4 and 6 are large. 3, 5 and 9 extend below the line, while the 7 goes below the line and then curls upward. Dates are uneven because of the size and position of the digits. Dwight used the old form of 's' and connected 'st' and 'ct', especially in the epitaphs (Fig. 8). His enthusiastic carving frequently took him to the edge of the tablet, with letters left over. To meet such situations, he simply made a bulge in the tablet or placed the word above. Dwight continued to fill orders for people in Dorchester. Among them is the stone for Miss Ruth Foster, 1783, daughter of the carver, James Foster III, who died in 1771, and his second wife, Mary (Fig. 7). It is much like the Metchel stone and has many of the idiosyncrasies discussed in that connection.

A type of face, previously used but never popular, appeared in the tympanum of a typical Dwight stone, that for James Locke of Ashby (1782) (Fig. 8). This face is oval, fat and "amiable." Dwight stopped using his mark with this change. Oval faces represented a short bridge from the earlier faces with narrow chins to a more modern pattern.

Fig. 7   Ruth Foster, 1783, Dorchester.

Fig. 8   James Locke, 1782, Ashby.

Another example of this change may be seen in the stone for Levi Gaschet (1784). This large stone tells the sad story of how Gaschet died when the Lord directed a tree to crush him to the ground (Fig. 9).

Of course change in styles did not come abruptly, with one type ending as the next began. This was an overlapping progression. Each new type became popular while stones in an earlier style were still being produced. Thus during the peak years of the Dwight workshop, the 1780s and 1790s, several different types of gravestone were being carved at the same time. A new pattern had its most popular period in the 1780s and is represented by the Edmond Morton stone (1786) (Fig. 10). The oval face is flanked by high, flat-carved wings, and is confined in a pod-shaped area. There are teardrops across the top of the pod and decorations below the wings that are familiar. There are no ribs on the feathers of Capt. Edmond Morton's wings. The side borders are a series of scrolls with teardrop lobes as a

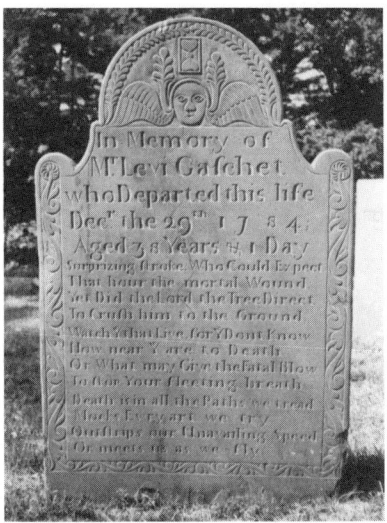

Fig. 9   Levi Gaschet, 1784, Townsend.

Fig. 10   Capt. Edmund Morton, 1786, Dorchester.

finial. The number 8 is smaller than the other numbers, as in Dwight's earlier stones. Thus some of the old characteristics continued, while others gave place to new.

Further changes appear on the stone for David Clap of Dorchester (Fig. 11), dated just one year later than the Morton stone. The oval head has a fringe of hair and is shaded by leaves -- the beginning of a series of designs that create an arch or crown effect. The shape of the tablet is different, dipping in the center and curving away from the shoulders, thus allowing more space for decoration without changing the shape of the stone. The 7 is now straight, the 't' looks normal, and the serifs on 'h' and 'l' are less pronounced.

Reading about the sequence of carving patterns and the transitional movement from one style to another can produce an artificial feeling of inevitability. Gravestone carving is a business, guided in the eighteenth century by the same principles that exist today. In the area of Massachusetts with which we are concerned, there was no lack of formidable competition. The Park family in Groton sold so many stones that it is difficult to find a graveyard in eastern Massachusetts in which they are not represented. John Dwight, with his smaller workshop, had to find ways in which to keep the shop open, through pricing, efficient production methods, product loyalty and the continual offering of new styles. These are modern words for an age-old truth.

When a change in style seems indicated, it is possible to look back and find a pattern element that can be augmented, re-styled and considered progressive. Perhaps brand new ideas were already budding. Sometimes the carver could satisfy the buyer only by adopting patterns of the competition, a perfectly legitimate practice. But it should be remembered that the carving of gravestones is also a craft, and examples could no doubt be shown where the craftsman has changed and developed patterns in areas where no competition existed.

Fig. 11   David Clap, 1787, Dorchester.

The stone in memory of the stillborn daughter of John and Susanna Dwight (1787) in Shirley initiates a series that persisted until the beginning of the nineteenth century and was among the more elaborate types carved in the Dwight workshop (Fig. 12). It is almost certain that John carved his daughter's gravestone. It shows a mixture of the old and the new elements. The round face with wings, now very popular, was often used by the Parks and shows their influence. The center lobe, of the original three, has evolved into an elongated, serrated leaf. Two leaves meet above the head, and elongated teardrops decorate the curve of the tablet. The wings have the expected ribs, and the feathers begin to separate at the bottom. The tablet has the old 's', short 't' and straight 7. A large 8 is used. The delicate drawings at the base, like a signature, are graceful versions of border designs no longer used.

Fig. 12   Daughter of John and Susanna Dwight, 1787, Shirley.

Fig. 13   Lieut. Elisha Rockwood, 1788, Groton.

Lieut. Elisha Rockwood's stone (1788) is another example of the new decorative styles initiated in the 1780s and chosen as memorials by many of Dwight's patrons (Fig. 13). The face with wings, free-floating, seems to look down from above, while wings sweep outward. The feathers are shorter. The outside feathers are ribbed, and the others stand out because the carving was now done in high relief. The tympanum has no complete border, and long leaves of a vine shade the head. The decoration, reaching down into the sides, is composed of familiar elements. Lieut. Elisha Rockwood's tablet gives only the important information and leaves space to appreciate the design. Sheaves with thin, opposed leaves begin in the center of the bottom border and continue up the sides, ending with a saw-tooth leaf at the top. The shape of the tablet has changed the appearance of the stone's typical shape. Some stones are less ornate than that of Elisha Rockwood, probably less expensive, but attractive in their simplicity. The rolled edging and inner plain band sets off the tablet which gives Lieut. Jeremiah Ball's name, lettered in italics, a major place on this smaller stone (1792). The face has wings that droop, and the outer feathers are ribbed (Fig. 14).

Most of John Dwight's stones of the type now under discussion have many of the same design elements and at a quick glance may look alike. But he included small differences in each. In the large Thomas Cowden stone (1792), for example, he used the same curled device under the face with wings as he used in the Jeremiah Ball stone of the same year and a similar design above the image (Fig. 15). The top of the tablet has an unusual shape, leaving room in the tympanum for columns which introduce architectural features to replace foliage in the pattern. Although the stone of Josiah How (Fig. 16) is again dated in the same year, 1792, as the Jeremiah Ball and Thomas Cowden stones, it is different in many details. The teardrops edge the stone completely, sparse foliage has a place in the corners, while bulging urns and tall columns make the face with wings look smaller, yet the face looks real and is well carved. The design is well balanced, again with thick columns to support the heavy tympanum.

Fig. 14 Lieut. Jeremiah Ball, 1792, Townsend.

Fig. 15   Thomas Cowden, 1792, Fitchburg.

Fig. 16   Deacon Josiah How, 1792, Milton.

As architectural designs became more popular, the face with wings began to go out of fashion. Patrons preferred the various new patterns which made use of the urn and willow, and the long period of creative carving in New England faded into the past. With the increased standardization of letters and numbers and the use of similar figures in the tympanum, designs came to look more alike, and the identity of the carver becomes more difficult to discover. On the other hand, the larger number of probated estates in the nineteenth century increases the possibility of finding a payment to the carver, thus documenting the stone and making easier the task of the researcher.

At the Dwight workshop, as in the shop of any stonecarver of the period, heavy work was necessary to prepare a stone before the master carver placed his chisel on its smooth surface. It is probable that John Dwight had apprentices, although no reference to them has been found. It is possible that John's stepson Abel Moors, who was about four years old when his mother married John Dwight and moved to the farm in Shirley, became a helper and perhaps later an apprentice in the shop. Abel was never adopted by John, and his uncle Joseph was appointed his guardian and later disqualified from managing his estate.[13] But it is certain that John's sons Francis, born in 1780, and Sullivan, born in 1785, assisted their father in his shop and later became master carvers themselves. In 1800 John turned the business over to Francis, then twenty years old. The turn of the century is therefore a good time to look at the Dwight family.

The Middlesex County census for 1800 lists in the Dwight household: 1 male, 10-16; 2 males, 16-26; 1 male over 45; 3 females 16-26; 2 females 26-45; 1 female over 45.[14] All John's children were still at home. Young John was graduated from Harvard College during this year and later became a successful doctor in Boston. Sullivan was then fifteen and working in his father's shop. He later opened a workshop of his own in Thomaston, Maine, in 1810, where he worked with marble, producing mantels and tabletops as well as gravestones. He married, had a family, and was respected by all who knew him. John's daughter Sally married Joseph Brown and moved to Westmoreland, New Hampshire, where he too carved gravestones. Their son, John Dwight Brown, followed the same profession.[15] One by one the other girls followed Sally in leaving the Dwight household.

With transfer of the business from John to his son Francis in 1800 the history of the Dwight workshop is largely a story of Francis and his work. He married Maria Blanchard of Jaffrey Center, New Hampshire, and brought her home to live at the farm. They had five children.[16] This was the sum of relevant information about the Dwight family until an exciting day for me in January 1986.

On that day the Librarian of the Hazen Memorial Library in Shirley spread before me a treasure discovered in the library archives. In folders were a deed to the house on the Mulpus, receipts, promissory notes, military records and orders for gravestones. It took days to read, transcribe and photocopy the out-dated handwriting, and to piece together the story of the last sixteen years in the lives of John and Francis Dwight.

A handwritten deed provides further evidence of a grant of quarry rights in Pin Hill from Daniel Hastings to John Dwight:

> Newton Feb.^{r} 27, 1800 --
> I the subscriber by these presents do quit and convey to Mr. John dwight of Shierley -- one half of the right of Diging Stones in the querry at Harvard which I bought or hyerd by lease of Mr. Jotham Barnard of sd. Harvard. (this I had leas'd to me and the Mr. Park's.)
> Daniel Hastings[17]

It is evident that Francis later rented other quarry rights at Pin Hill, for among the papers appears the following:

> Harvard May 12th 1815 Reciev'd of Francis Dwight three dollars & thirty three Cents it being in full for Quarry rent to this date
> Caleb Warner

Francis loved music, gave lessons, directed a band and knew how to repair instruments. In the inventory of his estate were: 1 clarinet, 1 singing book, Psalm book, bass viol. The inventory also listed: Uniform hat and feather, coat and Epaulet, vest, pantaloons, gaters and shoes and a sword with belt.[18] There is no way to know whether the uniform was for the band, the militia, or both. The militia, of which Lieut. Francis Dwight appeared to be second in command, met regularly to drill. There is an order for him to conduct the muster on Wednesday, next, and to command the company until the return of the Com.^{r} Joseph Edgerton.[19]

Francis continually borrowed from friends and relatives. There are many notes and about as many receipts for payment:

> Boston 14 April 1812 For value received I promise to pay John Dwight or order Ninety Dollars on demand with interest.
> Francis Dwight

> Shirley, March 5th 1813 Received of Francis Dwight five dollars in full of all Book accounts to this date.
> John Dwight

Creditors did want every cent due, but this was perhaps written with a smile:

> Shirley Nov. 27th 1809 Received one Cent in full of all Book accounts to this date of Francis Dwight. I say recev'd by me
> Daniel Kezar

An early order for a gravestone reads:

> Asa Farwell Junr was born April the 8th 1800 And died November the 11th 1814 a verse Price 5.00 to be done first haying to be paid in lumber

Asa's stone is at Laurel Hill cemetery in Fitchburg, overlooking the down-town area. It has a willow with urn and a lobed vine in the side borders. The stone shows only from the top to the date so we do not know what verse was used. And here is still another order:

> West Cambridge Mr Capt Stephen Frost Died. October 31. In the year 1810. Remember man is born to Die, His months are all with God; None from the stroke of Death can fly Or break his iron rod. Price from 12 to 15 dollars

West Cambridge is now Arlington, Massachusetts. The order for this stone went to the Dwight workshop but it was not carved by either John or Francis. The lettering and the pattern are done by a hand I do not recognize.

The Dwights had ties to Temple, New Hampshire, where they ordered a fine grade of "chees." And among the papers is this order:

> Francis Dwight the Stone Cutter Shirley, Mass. Temple June 27th 1816 Sir I would inform you that I want a pair of gravestones for my father Archelaus Cumings who Departed this life July fourth 1814 in the sixty third year of his age. I want good stones worth about 14 dollars I could not send before for I did not know the price of Stones. Letter them in the usual manner if you have the opportunity Send me word when they are done. To Francis Dwight
>
>   Arch. Cumings

The stone is still standing in the burying ground down the hill from the Center (Fig. 17). This stone, though it resembles those done by Francis Dwight, lacks many of the decorative details used by him. It has an oddity that suggests a different carver -- the figure 1 in the date has a semicircular serif visible in a rubbing (Fig. 17a) but not in a photograph. There are several other stones in the Temple graveyard like this and several others that do seem to have been done by Francis. The orders received by the Dwight workshop shortly before the death of John and Francis were very likely done by other carvers, possibly including Francis's brother Sullivan.

The only signed stone carved by Dwight that has been discovered is that of Susanna Bailey (1811) in Jaffrey Center, New Hampshire (Fig. 18). It is signed at the bottom: "Wrought by F. Dwight S" (Fig. 18 insert). This is a large and excellent stone of the urn and willow type. A narrow rope-like border outlines the stone, and the branches in the tympanum hang over the secondary border. The urn is typical of the Francis Dwight type. Notice the heart at the base of the bowl. The delicate twigs in the corners are also characteristic and occasionally used for dainty borders. The horizontal border of starred lozenges is typical. Sturdy columns form side borders and fans decorate corners of the tablet. The lettering is typical of the Dwight workshop, and the 2 was used only by Francis.

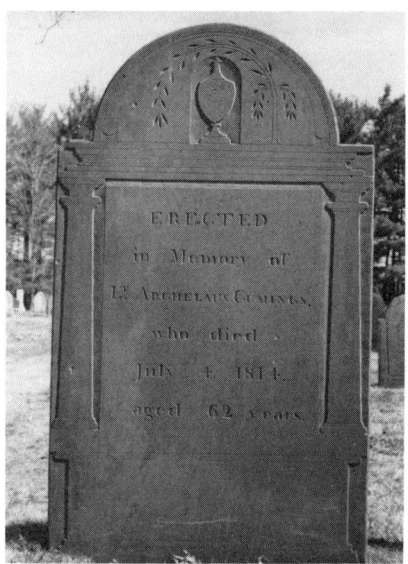

Fig. 17   Lt. Archelaus Cumings, 1814, Temple, NH.

Fig. 17a Detail from Cumings stone.

Fig. 18 Susanah Bailey, 1811, Jaffrey Center, NH.

Fig. 18a   Detail from Bailey stone.

On January 13, 1814 Francis entered into an agreement with his cousin, David Sawtell, described as a stonecutter of Groton, Massachusetts. The agreement recites that Sawtell had given Francis (described in this document as "Gentleman") four promissory notes, each in the amount of $312.50, payable in four successive years. The money had apparently been loaned by Francis to David, and the agreement gives David the right to cut slate from Francis's interest at Pin Hill, the slate so cut to be used for gravestones to be delivered to Francis and for "no other cause whatsoever." The agreement was accomplished by a series of real estate transactions: Francis deeded to David a parcel of land, with buildings, near Mulpus Brook, and "a small patch improved as a garden spot," in consideration of $1500. David mortgaged this land back to Francis as security for the notes and in consideration of $250 gave him a deed of a small tract of land in Groton near Ridge Hill Tavern. A little over a year later, on February 17, 1815, these transactions were in effect reversed. David gave up his right of redemption in the Mulpus Brook mortgage by a new deed to Francis. Francis deeded back the Ridge Hill Tavern piece to David for $250, and took from David a mortgage on this parcel to cover the purchase price. There is no record of a discharge of this mortgage, and so Francis was left in the end as the owner of both parcels.[20]

It appears from the Dwight papers that Sullivan did work for his brother Francis, for the papers include a bill for carving and lettering gravestones in a total amount of $15.78 for work on eleven stones. Charges were based on so much per foot of lettering, the greatest length being 10 1/2 feet, with a charge of $4.09. The bill does not indicate the year in which it was rendered, but presumably it was after Sullivan had set up for himself in Thomaston, Maine.

John Dwight sold the farm to Francis, May 15, 1815, for three thousand dollars. Susannah made her mark on the deed in relinquishment of her right of dower in the premises.[21] This took the estate and its benefits out of the inheritance of John's other children and made Francis and his family the beneficiaries. There is no record that the brothers and sisters were consulted. They may have had farms of their own and expected that, as was usual in that day, Francis and Maria would in return take care of their parents, keeping the farm and business going as usual.

But this was not to be. In the summer of the following year tragedy struck the Dwight family. The story is succinctly told in Chandler's *History of Shirley*:[22]

> "Within six weeks time, John Dwight and his wife, his son Francis and wife, all living under the same roof, died one after the other, having been poisoned by some corned beef of which they ate, that was diseased."

The family gravestones give the dates of death, shortly succeeding each other:

Fig. 19   John Dwight, 1816, Shirley.

Susanna Dwight died September 6, 1816
Francis Dwight died September 29, 1816
John Dwight died October 2, 1816   (Fig. 19)
Maria Dwight died October 9, 1816

Francis and Maria left five children, aged one to eleven years. The property was sold, and at the sale "20 ruff gravestones were purchased by William Brown" (perhaps a relative of John Dwight's son-in-law, Joseph Brown). John Dwight's workshop disappeared.

It has been said that a man can be judged by the values he admires in others. John Dwight's tribute "To the Memory of a Beloved Friend" also describes his own life:

"in his life he was a Kind & Loving Husband
a tender and Provident Parent
a friendly and Benevolent Neighbour;
Singularly Pitiful and Liberal,
to the Poor; Needy and Distressed
  his life useful
  his Death lamented."[23]

The John Dwight Workshop

Addendum - Painted Gravestones

The following recipe, found among the Dwight papers, has no date or other identification, but it was presumably written in the early 1800s. It adds a little evidence to the small store of knowledge on a subject which has thus far had little exploration -- the painting of gravestones in the eighteenth and early nineteenth centuries:

> This is written for Francis Dwight pleas to hand it to him Capt. Dwight To one quart of oile boile it with red led thirely then put in resin the bigness of an ounce Leatherage gold an ounce apeace of white viteral white led the bigness of an egg ground and stird in after cool mix your paint thick and paint but once draw your brush up and down the stone keep your stones in the shop turn the back out and if you boil it well they will dry in 2 or 3 days fit for use and you may see your face in them it will not do to dry them in the sun have your paint warm when you put it on[24]

The recipe is very similar to an entry dated February 17, 1801 in a cabinet maker's apprentice handbook "for Boiling of oil":

> take red led white viteral litherage one ounce of each and three ounces of rosin to one gallon of oil. red led Put in when the oil is boiling prevents it burning. White must be put in when the oil is taken off and sturred untill the oil is Cold.[25]

In both entries the initial instructions are for making an oil base. The red lead is not a coloring agent. And as appears in both entries, the paint pigments are to be added after the oil has cooled.[26]

But it is clear from the Dwight recipe that its objective was the use of paint in some fashion on gravestones. Kevin Sweeney, writing of Samuel Dougherty, a Whately, Massachusetts, carver active from 1806 until about 1836, has this to say:

> On 30 December 1806, Dougherty placed an advertisement in the *Hampshire Gazette* announcing that he "has commenced painting and stonecutting business." It is unclear from the advertisement if

Eloise Sibley West

Dougherty painted gravestones or was a house painter in addition to becoming a stonecutter. Contemporary documents and physical evidence on Plymouth County, Massachusetts, gravestones suggest that a few early nineteenth-century gravestones were actually painted. The stones may have been polychromed or perhaps painted white to resemble marble if they were slate or the painting may have involved nothing more than a coloring of the inscription to make it more legible.[27]

James and Donna Belle Garvin, writing of the New Hampshire carver Stephen Webster (1717/18-1798), have this to say:

Some of Stephen Webster's gravestones also suggest another possibility. They may originally have been painted. Several of those in the Chester and Hollis cemeteries bear traces of what appears to be black and red pigment. The black, particularly, is generally seen only in the deeply incised portions of the stones, especially in the lettering. If Webster enriched the already brilliant patterns of his stones with paint, the effect must have been startling indeed. The traces of color on these stones suggest a new image of eighteenth century mortuary art, and should alert researchers elsewhere to the possible uses of paint in early graveyards.[28]

The practice of coloring stones was also known in Connecticut. In writing of carver John Dolph (1776-1815) Ernest Caulfield quotes from the Connecticut probate records:

May 31st 1803. Two Cash paid Dolph for Grave Stones 0.15.0
June 27 Two cash paid for colouring said stones 0.3.0.

Caulfield adds in a footnote that in the probate papers of Daniel Barker of Branford there is a similar item: "payed Jonathan palmer one shilen for Culering Daniel Barkers grave stones 0.1.0".[29]

In Caulfield's own copy of this article (in the possession of Dr. James Slater) is handwritten in ink the following:

Oscar Ogg the 26 Letters Crowell co. N.Y. 1958 page 109 After the outlines (of the letters) had been carved out carefully with the chisel, they were gone over and filled with paint to make them look like the original writing' (Talking about the early Romans)[30]

Here, then, in the papers of Francis Dwight is an intriguing note which bears evidence that he, among other stonecarvers of the time, added color to his work. This is a subject which warrants far more research!

Editor

NOTES

The author wishes to thank the following persons: Mrs. Elizabeth Wade, Librarian of Hazen Memorial Library, Shirley, Mass. and Mrs. Meredith Marcinkewicz for use of the original Dwight Papers that form an important part of this study; the Shirley Town Clerk, Mrs. Sylvia Shipton, for use of the original Town Records and other official information; Daniel and Jessie Farber for the Farber collection of gravestone photographs now available for study through photocopies, upon request from the Research Co-ordinator of the Association for Gravestone Studies; (the photographs for this article were made by the author, except that of Deacon Josiah How, which was done by Laurel K. Gabel); and Theodore Chase for finding and describing the real estate transactions between Francis Dwight and David Sawtell and for preparing the Addendum. My special thanks also to Mrs. Gabel, Research Co-ordinator for the AGS. Her information, assistance and encouragement have made this study possible.

1. Harriette M. Forbes, *Gravestones of Early New England and the Men Who Made Them 1653-1800* (Boston: Houghton Mifflin, 1927; rpt. Princeton, NJ: The Pyne Press, 1955; New York: DaCapo, 1967), 79.

2. Benjamin W. Dwight, *The History of the Descendants of John Dwight of Dedham, Mass.* 2 vols. (New York: John F. Trow and Son, 1814), 2:1011. Information given by Priscilla Cowdery, a daughter of the carver John Dwight, to Benjamin W. Dwight in 1866, when she was 84 years old. Dwight, *Descendants*, 2:1011.

3. Seth Chandler, *History of the Town of Shirley, Massachusetts* (Shirley, Mass.: Published by the Author, 1883), 391.

Eloise Sibley West

4. Chandler, *History of Shirley*, 563.

5. *Vital Records of Shirley, Massachusetts to the Year 1850* (Boston: The New England Historic and Genealogical Society, 1918), 69. This information is also reported in the *Records of the First Parish Church of Shirley* and in the *Shirley Town Records of Birth, Marriages and Deaths 1753-1850*, available at the office of the Shirley Town Clerk.

6. *Shirley Town Business 1753-1853* (Shirley, Mass.: Office of the Town Clerk; records hand-copied from the originals). In the record of marriages in the Office of the Town Clerk, page 150 showing the marriage of Susanna and John Dwight is torn and the date lost. In Dwight's *Descendants* the name is Moore, 2:1011.

7. Middlesex Co. Deeds 70:123. Ethel S. Bolton, *Shirley Uplands and Intervales* (Boston: George Emery Littlefield, 1914),253: List of owners of the John Dwight farm on Town Meeting Road, Shirley, Mass.

8. *Massachusetts Soldiers and Sailors of the Revolutionary War* (Boston: Wright & Potter, 1899), 109; and Chandler's *History of Shirley*, 391.

9. *Town Records of Town of Shirley, Mass. 1754-1810*, 2 vols. (Publ. by the Town of Shirley, Mass.). The earliest pages are not numbered. 1:64.

10. *Shirley Town Business*, 130.

11. *Town Records of Shirley*, Vol. 1, March 14, 1777 entry.

12. Middlesex Co. Probate files 10651 and 6604. For a description of quarrying methods see Henry D. Nourse, *History of the Town of Harvard, Massachusetts 1732-1893* (Harvard , MA, printed for Warren Hapgood, 1893), 70, 450.

13. Middlesex Co. Probate file 15375.

14. National Archives, Waltham, Mass., 1800 Census, Middlesex County, Shirley, Mass., John Dwight 01201, p. 213.

15. Dwight, *Descendants*, 2:1013.

16. Dwight, *Descendants*, 2:1016.

17. Hazen Memorial Library, Shirley, Mass., the Library file for Dwight. All the following indented material are quotations from this file unless separately noted.

18. Middlesex Co. Probate file 6600. The inventory of real estate includes a Tavern House with buildings estimated at $700.

19. *Military Orders* in Dwight file, Shirley Town Library.

20. The agreement is in the Shirley Library file. David Sawtell married Lucy Dickerson, daughter of Priscilla (Harris) Dickerson, who was a sister of Susanna Dwight, mother of Francis. Chandler, *History of Shirley*, 388. The deeds covering the land near Mulpus Brook are recorded with Middlesex Co. Deeds 207:1, 209:9 and 211:54; and those covering the land near Ridge Hill Tavern in 209:9, 211:192 and 211:51. Both John and Francis Dwight engaged in numerous other real estate transactions as an examination of the grantor and grantee indices at the Middlesex Country Registry of Deeds will readily show.

21. Middlesex Co. Deeds 215:525.

22. Chandler, *History of Shirley*, 391.

23. The gravestone of Hezekiah Sawtell (1739), Groton, Mass. (Fig. 5).

24. The Library file of Dwight papers also includes: "A receipt to make Liquid Blacking - Take one fourth of an ounce of Oil of Vitriol, one fourth of a pound of Ivory black, one gill of sweet oil, one ditto of molasses, one quart of vinegar. Mix the first four articles together into a consistency, then add the vinegar which will cause high fomentation and in twelve hours it will be fit for use."

25. *Bulletin of the Connecticut Historical Society*, (January, 1943), Vol. 9, No. 2, p. 16.

26. The quotation from the cabinetmaker's handbook and the reference to the stonecarver Samuel Dougherty which follows were brought to the editor's attention by Kevin M. Sweeney, Director of Academic Programs at Historic Deerfield, Inc. The opinion as to the use of the recipe written for Dwight was expressed by William Flynt, architectural conservator at Historic Deerfield.

27. *The Great River: Art & Society of the Connecticut Valley, 1635-1820* (Hartford: Wadsworth Athenaeum, 1985) #351. Ludwig suggests that many of the early nineteenth century neoclassical stones in Plymouth County look as if they had been polychromed. Allen I. Ludwig, *Graven Images* (Middletown, CT: Wesleyan Univ. Press, 1966), 337.

28. *Historical New Hampshire* (Summer, 1974), Vol. 29, No. 2, p. 102.

29. Ernest Caulfield, "Connecticut Gravestones X," *The Connecticut Historical Society Bulletin* (January, 1965), Vol. 30, No. 1, p. 17.

30. Letter from Dr. Slater to the editor dated December 29, 1987.

Fig. 1   Othello, 1818, Harvard, Mass.

TRIBUTES IN STONE AND LAPIDARY LAPSES: COMMEMORATING BLACK PEOPLE IN EIGHTEENTH- AND NINETEENTH-CENTURY AMERICA

Angelika Krüger-Kahloula

> Laid to rest in a "potter's field," the dead bodies of the slaves never mingle their dust with that of the sovereign race. No monument, inscribed with the name of the deceased, ever marks the spot where he lies, as no legal sanction was ever given to his name while he lived. A rough stone, gathered from the wayside, or a branch of cedar, soon to die, is his only monument. So perish, an undistinguishable throng, the enslaved race of the South.[1]

This remark on the absence of lasting memorials holds true for the vast majority of antebellum African Americans. It is the exceptional gravemarkers erected to the memory of black individuals in eighteenth- and nineteenth-century America with which this paper is concerned.[2] Many of the grave inscriptions evoke similar themes. In their attempt to define the social distinction of the deceased and to describe the loss experienced by surviving contemporaries, those who commissioned the stones drew upon a store of concepts of what African Americans ought to be in relation to their family or friends, employers or masters. The epitaphs project ideal images of men and women that reflect the expectations of American society toward its black members.

In terms of predominance, memorials offered white patrons the last opportunity to define black identities. The moral values chiselled in stone resemble those upheld in addresses and in the literature of the period: faithfulness and dedication are highly praised in domestics, justice between the races is deferred to a future state of existence, black people's family attachments are blithely ignored or downgraded in competition with their ties to employers or masters. The first four sections of this paper, each assembling epitaphs that make a certain point and sometimes employ similar phrases, present inscriptions that exemplify the values mentioned above. The next two sections raise the question of how personhood and chattel slavery, devalued status and esteem are made to agree in certain inscriptions. In several of the epitaphs assembled in the last three sections the deceased seems to gain his/her own voice. They depict reversals of fortune, sometimes tied to geographic transition. Africa is mentioned as a counterplace to America.

Blacks were not the only group in America whose members fell into historic oblivion at or soon after death. Only a minority of the population was able to afford costly stone markers that preserved biographical information for posterity. Unfortunately, African American genealogical and historical research using epitaphic evidence has to reckon with the selection exercised by slaveholders as a determining factor, in addition to those of class, gender, and generation, which usually influence the size of monuments and the material used. Considering the conspicuous absence of tombstones erected for the underprivileged in American cemeteries and abroad, the relative frequency of markers commemorating "faithful servants" in early black American cemeteries is striking. If one is to believe the epitaphs, a large proportion of eighteenth- and nineteenth-century African Americans were docile domestics.

In addition to the selective factors which determine the recording of black lives on tombstones, we need to keep in mind the generally elusive character of African American vital statistics during slavery. Each change of owner implied a possible change of name and date of birth for a slave if the seller made age adjustments for better marketing. One slave narrative voices the baffled attempt at resolving such data:

> When in Slavery, I was called Fed. Why I was so named, I cannot tell. I never knew myself by any other name, nor always by that; for it is common for slaves to answer to any name, as it may suit the humour of the master. I do not know how old I am, but think I may be any age between thirty-five and forty.[3]

The epitaphs presented and discussed here are meant to offer an introduction to black American grave inscriptons. This paper cannot pretend to provide a comprehensive survey, nor even a representative one, as the basic data are literally fragmentary and scattered. Stones for blacks are not countless, but are as yet uncounted. They are not untraceable, but hard to trace.

Some of the inscriptions are curious, yet they are not isolated curios. Placed in a socio-historical perspective they contribute to our understanding of interethnic relations in eighteenth- and nineteenth-century America. The leading question is: Who was commemorated and for what reasons? In the case of markers put up by masters for slaves one may note the contradictory nature of the act: erecting a tombstone authenticated the slaves's existence and acknowledged him or her as a person in spite of his/her legal definition as chattel and the assertion of ownership in the epitaph. At the same time, their chattel status reflected slaves as property in wills and inventories of estates.

The erection of a monument honors the deceased interred beneath it. But how can a slave, a person who is socially dishonored by definition, be honored? Orlando Patterson, who has explored the psychosocial implications of slavery, points to the lack of reciprocity in master-slave relationships:

> And while they may have been greatly honored by their doting masters, none of these slaves were in themselves honorable persons.... And though honored, and no doubt craving honor, none of them were ever able to bestow honor or to confirm it, at least not to anyone who mattered.[4]

What sounds like a linguistic play on words is the consequence of crass social imbalance. As a result of this imbalance, the mere fact that a white person raised a gravemarker for a black person conferred posthumous honor on the latter.

An inscription such as the following from Cobb County, Georgia, was probably meant to enhance the reputation of the deceased:

> This stone is dedicated to the memory of Trupe McClesky, col. by one of his white friends. d. Jan. 1916, aged 92 yrs.[5]

Even in this century, the decision of the "white friend" to remain anonymous is a rare act of modesty--unless it was prompted by fear of white opprobrium.

Other donors of memorials used the opportunity to advertize their charity. And the public received the message. When visiting a New Orleans cemetery in the early nineteenth century, Timothy Flint came across a "plain but respectable" gravemarker erected "as a grateful record of the long, faithful, and affectionate services of a black slave."[6] Flint's comment furnishes a clue to the motives underlying the purchase of the gravestone:

> The whole inscription wears a delightful simplicity, and honours the master that erected it, as much as the slave.[7]

Memorials for slaves were a convenient medium for advertising ideal images of both servants and masters. Not only the inscription but also the type of stone used, as well as the skill and time spent in working it, indicate the "worth" of the deceased for the survivors.[8]

Self-aggrandizing portrayal of masters on servants' tombstones is not, however, restricted to American slaveholders. Kenneth Lindley observes a similar tendency in British servants' epitaphs. He notes that "it was usual for the employer to include his or her own name on the stone, often in larger letters than the name of the servant commemorated."[9] The qualities mentioned most frequently on the British stones compare with those on black American ones: "faithful," "zealous," and "honest."[10] The custom of commemorating servants was widespread enough for a book of epitaphs to "Faithful Servants" to be published in Britain as late as 1891. It contained 700 examples.

While the majority of epitaphs commissioned by slaveholders concealed or obfuscated the reality of dependence and oppression, masters unwittingly or intentionally left a memorial to themselves and to the social and cultural hegemony they practiced. Given that most gravestones are not designed or even chosen by the person they commemorate but by the survivors, the stones tend to tell as much about the latter as the former.

Epitaphs are notably euphemistic and eulogistic, but they tend to uphold social distinctions. In the case of African American slaves, explicit or implicit references to ethnicity and status such as "slave of," "property of," or "Negro servant of," the choice of a gravemarker of inferior size and quality or grave location in a segregated or marginal area are indicators of subordinate position. Conversely, a marker of average size and quality situated in the central part of the grounds, with an inscription and ornamental design that do not identify the ethnic origin of the deceased (although the name may), would signify equal status among the interred of that particular cemetery.[11]

As opposed to Christian concepts of postmortem existence, many traditional African religions do not envision individual resurrection at some future date. Rather they see a continuation of life in the world of the ancestors, which often mirrors the world of the living in its social and economic concerns. A deceased individual is assured survival as long as the living remember him/her in their thoughts and in their rites. In African traditional thought the interdependence of the living and the dead is taken for granted. The exchange of services between the two ensures harmony and well-being. The grave is a place where the two worlds meet and where communication between them can be established. In various cultures the everyday contact with the dead is held via sculptures placed in the village rather than at the cemeteries, which are of difficult access in the bush. In others, objects placed on the grave are of great symbolic and ritualistic value in holding dialogue with the ancestors. This does not necessarily render gravemarkers superfluous. In their study of recent Ivory Coast funeral monuments Susan Domovitz and Renzo Mandirola write:

> For the Anyi and the Brong, to be forgotten is far worse than death. The grave monument is an attempt to survive death, to survive the possibility of being forgotten. Like the funeral ceremony, it is a message addressed to two worlds: it is a letter of recommendation to the ancestors in the next world, and in this world a bid for immortality, a confirmation of worldly success.[12]

It is the bid for immortality in this world with which the American memorials to be studied are concerned. They will be interpreted as expressions of interethnic rather than interpersonal or intragroup relationships. The epitaphs vary in documentary and expressive quality. While some use conventional memorial expressions and probably take their inspiration from monument makers' manuals, others are unique compositions, and still others, though written on the death of a particular individual, echo sentiments and phrases without copying the exact wording.

Free At Last, A Faithful Friend

One slaveholding doctrine held that only death could terminate slavery, and this is also a part of Christian doctrine. The entry for May 14, 1821, of a plantation diary records the death of "Old Bina." It reads like an epitaph: "She is now a free woman. Her virtues were numerous and her vices such as arose from her station in life."[13] A grave inscripton from South Carolina also refers to a future state of freedom, listing first the servile qualities cherished in the deceased:

> JOHN:
> A FAITHFUL SERVANT
> AND TRUE FRIEND:
> KINDLY, AND CONSIDERATE:
> LOYAL, AND AFFECTIONATE:
> THE FAMILY HE SERVED
> HONOURS HIM IN DEATH:
> BUT, IN LIFE, THEY GAVE HIM LOVE:
> FOR HE WAS ONE OF THEM.
> THERE SHALL BE NEITHER BOND NOR SLAVE[14]

Reference to a future existence provides a perspective that neutralizes the incongruous categories of slave and friend. In all probability the author of the epitaph was unaware of the ambiguity inherent in the last statement: would there be no bond of friendship between John and his master in the hereafter?

Love in life, honor in death: the reader of the epitaph is left with the impression that money in remuneration for rendered services would be too base a compensation. Nor is John in need of a family name, given his close family attachment. Genovese has noted the abundance of references to the slave force as "the black family" in the written records of the antebellum South.[15] Even in the 1930s a Southerner asserts: "If a gentleman said 'my negroes' there was no more arrogance intended than when he spoke of his home and family."[16] The authors of *Deep South* caution against such declarations:

> When white employers say that a colored servant is a "part of the family," they never indicate that she is no longer considered as lower caste. They mean, rather, that she has a definite and very strong position as a servant in the family life, a position such that she has very intimate and emotional relations with the members of the family and with their home.... The fundamental caste structure of the relationships between her and her white adult employers remains, however.[17]

From the employees' point of view, domestic service usually entails the surrender of individual autonomy and of a family life of their own.[18] When divested of the exploitative aspect, on the other hand, loyalty to an employer, which also means steady employment, is not disdained.[19]

If the pronouns in such phrases as "my negroes" or "our people" are meant to convey a sense of belonging and attachment, they also affirm ownership. Possessive paternalism survives in twentieth-century memorials such as the following:

> To
> the glory of God
> and in affectionate
> remembrance of all
> our people at
> BELVIDERE
> PLANTATION
> WHO ARE IN GOD'S
> SAFE KEEPING, THIS
> CEMETERY HAS BEEN GIVEN
> by
> Caroline S. Sinkler
> Emily W. Roosevelt
> Anne W. Fishburne
> Caroline S. Lockwood
> JAN. 1941
> "I know that my
> Redeemer liveth"[20]

Whereas the names of the philanthropic women are listed individually, the black servants who have exchanged keepers are recorded as a group, not even in their own right and name but as "all our people."

The affirmations of friendship and affection found in grave inscriptons may sometimes be taken at face value. In December 1785 Henry Bromfield, born in Boston, was living in the village of Harvard, Massachusetts.

Commemorating Black People

He had just lost his second wife. He wrote to his brother in England: "I am solus here, except a negro man." This was the faithful Othello, of whom it was later written:[21]

> Everyone, man, woman and child in Harvard, and I may say the surrounding county, knew this excellent and devoted servant. Born a slave, he was in the employ of Mr. Bromfield for many years. Several anecdotes are told of his eccentricities, and of the entire dependence that the master had upon the servant. He died about seven years before Mr. Bromfield. Buried in an obscure corner of the graveyard, his resting place was neglected, and almost unknown until marked by a neat stone, erected by the late Henry B. Pearson, Esq., with the following inscription upon it (Figs. 1 and 2).
>
> Othello
> The Faithful Friend of
> Henry Bromfield
> Came from Africa About 1760,
> Died 1813, Aged About 72.[22]

Fig. 2 Othello's grave in a corner of the Harvard burying ground.

Angelika Krüger-Kahloula

In earlier years masters were less reluctant to indicate both affection and status, as in the following inscription from Newport, Rhode Island:

> In Memory
> of Pompey
> Beloved Servt
> of Josias
> Lyndon
> who died Sept
> 11 1765 Aged
> 28 M^o and
> 9 Days.

A Southern slaveholder may have been hesitant to employ the term "friend" for fear of undermining the caste system, although some pro-slavery literature provided models of affective patterns in the doting master and the devoted slave. Writing in 1856 a Northern traveller captures some of the intricacies of paternalism in the declaration made by a slave owner at the death of a favorite servant:

> I lost this morning the truest and most reliable friend I had in the world, one whom I have been accustomed to honor and respect since my earliest recollection; he was the playmate of my father's youth, and the Mentor of mine; a faithful servant, an honest man, and a sincere Christian.[23]

Neither the Southern speaker nor the reporter (whose pseudonym "Viator" betrays training in the classics and who can therefore be assumed to be familiar with the role of slave educators in ancient Greece) sees anything incongruous in a slave playmate or mentor. The last three phrases of the quotation might come straight from an epitaph.

The deceased slave is said to have been honored and respected during life. Other texts present paternalistic relationships in which affection is all too obviously offered as a substitute for respect, and sentimentality is supposed to compensate for lack of justice. Susan D. Smedes tells of a master's attachment to an old slave woman, whom he has buried without a funeral sermon because he does not know anyone good enough to preach the sermon.[24] Apparently the idea of choosing a preacher whom the woman's kin or friends deem adequate does not occur to him. He also declares that "he would be proud to hang her portrait in his drawing-room, in such esteem and affection did he hold her."[25] The subjunctive mood indicates that he failed to have her picture painted, so her likeness never graced his walls.

Class demarcations are upheld while the socially superior display conspicuous compassion for the inferior. Self-styled "Southern matron" Caroline Gilman unwittingly exposes the discrepancy between (socially gratuitous) emotional grief and (distinction-conferring) formal mourning on the occasion of the death of a favorite domestic.

> We were a mourning family; true, we were not clad in weeds, but a tender tie had been riven, and it was riven with tears. None but those who live under our peculiar institutions can imagine the strong bond existing between faithful servants and the families with whom they are connected.[26]

For the Victorian reading public the image of the tie riven with tears may indeed have held more appeal than that of crepe clothing. Yet, for their social equals, Victorians indulged heavily in private and in public mourning.

The grave inscription chosen for the cherished servant is as follows:

SACRED
To the memory of
J A C Q U E ,
a faithful slave.
His master bears this testimony to his worth.[27]

Angelika Krüger-Kahloula

The use of the term "worth" in the epitaph of a person who, during his lifetime, was subject to sale, and whose market value could be determined by any slave dealer, appears rather awkward, although one may safely assume that no irony or punning was intended.

Model Men and Women

In the following inscription the word "worth" lends itself to less speculation since it is syntactically equivalent to other character qualities.

> To record the worth, fidelity and virtue of Reynolda Watts, (who died on the 2d day of May 1829 at the age of 24 years, in giving birth to her 3d child). Reared from infancy by an affectionate mistress and trained by her in the paths of virtue. She was strictly moral in her deportment, faithful and devoted in her duty and heart and soul a....[28]

Sand having drifted over the remainder when Olmsted visited the black Savannah cemetery in 1853, we are left to puzzle over Reynolda Watts's further moral attributes--which, according to this portrayal, are matched by those of her mistress.

If we are to believe the grave inscriptions, there was an extraordinarily high percentage of paragons of virtue among the population of eighteenth- and nineteenth-century America. Epitaphs of all periods and places tend to eulogize; eighteenth-century epitaphs use many words to do it. Almost all of the lengthy inscriptions we find in old burying grounds belong to the graves of well-to-do white Americans, but some African Americans were thus memorialized as well.

The longest inscription Olmsted copied in Savannah, that of Baptist pastor Andrew Brian, contains almost three hundred words. The biographical part describes his dedication to preaching the gospel and his willingness to die a martyr. It concludes: "He was an honour to human nature an ornament to religion and a friend to mankind." The memoir is followed by a poem on tranquil death, a scriptural passage, and the tribute: "This stone is erected by the First Colored Church as a token of love for their most faithful pastor. A.D. 1821."[29]

Obviously the epithet "faithful" is not restricted to a combination with "servant" or to persons of African descent. It takes on different connotations when used with social roles that are undertaken voluntarily. Two antebellum epitaphs for white Southerners, a man and a woman, may be presented for comparative purposes.

William Harris is buried in Marietta, Georgia. He lived from 1780 to 1857. His epitaph reads:

> He early in youth attached himself
> to the M.E. Church, lived and died
> an acceptable member. He was faith-
> ful and exemplary in all the rela-
> tions of husband, parent, and master.
> When a young man he served in the
> legislature of Georgia from Jones
> County. He was an emphatically
> honest man. The noblest work of
> God.[30]

True to the ideal of reciprocity of services and care in the master-slave relationship, the master can be characterized as "faithful" as well. Slavery is treated as an extension of patriarchy. Whereas a slave might be characterized as "honest," too, the expression "emphatically honest" implies a degree of moral force and self-determination that can hardly be attributed to a person deprived of free will.

In the epitaph of the white woman, Elizabeth Freeman of Plymouth, Massachusetts, identity is also determined by marital status and maternal role. The inscription stresses the sense of personal loss felt by her family rather than expanding upon her virtues. The fact that she was a minister's wife may have made references to piety or charity superfluous. More important in the choice of inscription was probably the nineteenth-century tendency to regard the death of a loved one as personal tragedy rather than God-willed fate.

> In memory of
> ELIZABETH
> wife of the
> REV. FREDERICK FREEMAN
> who died
> March 12, 1833
> aged 33 yrs.
> Leaving her husband and
> five children to deplore
> their loss, and cherish the
> dear remembrance of
> her worth.
> "Her children rise up and call
> her blessed; her husband also
> and he praiseth her."[31]

Nancy Williams, black domestic in the Freeman household, had died less than two years before her mistress. Her epitaph refers to her humble social position, which is taken for granted.

> In
> memory of
> NANCY WILLIAMS
> a faithful (African) servant
> in the family of
> Rev. F. Freeman.
> died Nov. 21. 1831,
> aged 25 years.
> "Honour and shame from no condition rise:
> Act well your part; --there all the honour lies."[32]

The memory of Nancy Williams is bound to occupational status and to ethnicity, not to family or matrimonial ties. The admonitory lines at the end, correlated with the information that Nancy Williams was an African servant, can hardly be read other than as a message to black Americans to "know their place" and to make the best of their assigned, subordinate position.

Exceptional Dedication

Epitaphs such as the following one from Newport, Rhode Island, praise the deceased for exceptionally long terms of service in one family.

> PORTSMOUTH
> Serv. of Mr DAVID
> CHESEBROUGH
> for more than Forty
> Years died June
> 19th 1772 aged
> about 57 years

A bronze tablet on a base of tabby (a traditional Georgian building material consisting of lime and gravel or shells) in Retreat Burying Ground, now located on the Sea Island Golf Course, tells the following story:

> NEPTUNE SMALL
> SEPTEMBER 15, 1831
> AUGUST 10, 1907
>
> NEPTUNE BELONGED TO MR. AND MRS. THOMAS BUTLER KING OF RETREAT / PLANTATION. WHEN THEIR SON CAPT. H.L.P. KING ENLISTED IN THE / CONFEDERATE ARMY NEPTUNE ACCOMPANIED HIM AS HIS BODY / SERVANT. CAPT. KING WAS KILLED IN THE BATTLE OF FREDERICKSBURG, / VIRGINIA, DECEMBER 13, 1862. WHEN NIGHT FELL NEPTUNE WENT OUT / ON THE BATTLEFIELD, FOUND THE BODY OF HIS MASTER AND BROUGHT / IT HOME TO REST IN THE FAMILY BURYING GROUND AT CHRIST CHURCH, / FREDERICA, ST. SIMONS ISLAND.

Angelika Krüger-Kahloula

The monument purports to commemorate Neptune Small. It marks the place where he is buried. The inscription also indicates the location of Small's former master's grave. It reports Small's loyalty and heroism. It also reports his former master's loyalty to the South and his heroic death. The first sentence of the short biography defines Small's identity as property of the Kings. The last sentence ends with their place of burial. When Small is mentioned in the text, only his first name is given. If it were not for the first line, written in large capital letters, the casual passer-by (such as a golfer looking for the ninth hole) might conclude that the monument was erected for King rather than Small. The first name by which Captain King was known was "Lord." Small is said to have chosen his self-effacing surname because of his small stature.[33]

A black person's readiness to defend the property of white people was appreciated and publicized by the white community. The type of the "faithful slave" ready to risk his/her life or health for his/her master which appears occasionally on tombstones is a stock character in literature about slavery. One-time sacrifice or service to the white community is more glamorous than life-long toil in the fields or kitchen.[34]

The Afro-American Historical and Cultural Museum in Philadelphia has a rubbing of the gravemarker of Dinah of Stenton:

> In memory of
> DINAH
> the
> Faithful Colored Caretaker
> of Stenton
> who by her quick thought
> and presence of mind
> saved the mansion
> from being burned
> by British soldiers
> in the winter of 1777.

Commemorating Black People

In Greenwood Cemetery, Brunswick, Georgia, a gravestone commemorates Stephen Wright, who also saved white property.

> This tribute in stone is raised
> by the citizens of Brunswick
> to mark the resting place of
> STEPHEN WRIGHT
> who lost his life
> in saving the property of
> his white fellow citizens
> in the great conflagration
> in Brunswick Georgia
> Nov. 16, 1884.
> His was a deed of heroism
> which the earthly historian
> will leave unnoticed
> But the records of heaven
> will perpetuate.

A rather dubious service to the community was rendered by Lydia Clark in nineteenth-century Delaware. Her solitary marker near Lewes reads:

> In memory of
> LYDIA CLARK
> Who died Dec. 26, 1856
> Aged about 75 years.
> The last one of the Aborigines
> of the Country, a person of
> truth and a witness against
> the arrogant Negros that
> assumed the be what they
> ware not.[35]

The monument is said to have been erected by Nathaniel Burton, a member of a local planter family, out of gratitude for testimony she gave in 1855. Burton accused a "Moor" storekeeper of possessing a gun and of selling ammunition to a free mulatto. "Moor" was an ethnic category not recognized by the federal government but by the state of Delaware, which allowed for a "Moor" school to be run in the Lewes area, in addition to a white, a black, and a native American one. People who designated themselves "Moors" claimed their descent from shipwrecked Spanish sailors who had intermarried with Indian women. They refused to be classified as African Americans, despite physical characteristics that suggested such descent. Lydia Clark testified that the "Moors" descended from an Irish woman who, before the Revolution, bought a black slave from a ship in Lewes. She had several children by him. They intermarried with Nanticoke Indians.[36]

The fact that Lydia Clark put partly black people into the ethnic slot allotted to them by the white community earned her a gravemarker. It is a monument to her and to the racial caste system. Both Lydia Clark and Dinah of Stenton have won official recognition by the Colonial Dames.

Whereas Wright, Small, Clark, and Dinah were memorialized by whites for specific services they rendered, Prince Hall and Pierre Toussaint have been celebrated by the black and the white public for exemplary service to the community. The grave of Prince Hall, the founder of black American Freemasonry, is marked by two monuments in Copp's Hill Burial Ground. The newer memorial, a broken column of polished stone, towers over a pair of gray tombstones that read:

Here Lies Ye Body of SARAH RITCHERY wife of PRINCE HALL Died Feby. the 26th 1769 Aged 24 years.	Here lies ye body of PRINCE HALL first Grand Master of the colored Grand Lodge of Masons in Mass. Died Dec. 7, 1807

Sources differ on Prince Hall's biography, but it is commonly held that he and fourteen other free blacks were initiated into Masonry by an army lodge of a British regiment in Boston on March 6, 1775.[37] The subsequently formed "African Lodge" was granted a charter from England on September 29, 1784.[38]

In spite of Masonic teaching of universal brotherhood, American lodges maintained the caste system. Only for special occasions such as the 1800 Masonic funeral ceremonies for George Washington or the 1850 anniversary celebration of the Bunker Hill battle did black and white lodges coordinate their procedures.[39]

Prince Hall's Masonic funeral was attended by black and white Bostonians. Eighty-eight years after his death a new monument, carrying the Masonic emblems, was unveiled in a ceremony in which Mason celebrities from different countries participated. The governor of Massachusetts reviewed the procession; the ensuing banquet took place at Faneuil Hall.[40]

Another memorable black man who rendered charitable services to blacks and whites has been honored by the Roman Catholic Church. A memorial plaque in Old Saint Patrick's churchyard on Mulberry Street, New York City, reads:

PIERRE TOUSSAINT
BORN A SLAVE IN
ST. MARK, SANTO DOMINGO, 1766
DIED IN NEW YORK CITY
JUNE 30, 1853

A CATHOLIC NEGRO LAYMAN
RESPECTED AND REVERED FOR
THE INTEGRITY OF HIS LIFE
AND FOR HIS MANY WORKS
OF CHARITY. A MEMBER OF
ST. PETER'S PARISH FOR 66 YEARS.

Angelika Krüger-Kahloula

> THIS TABLET AFFIXED
> SUNDAY, JULY 1, 1951, BY
> THE JOHN BOYLE O'REILLY COMMITTEE
> FOR INTERRACIAL JUSTICE.

According to a booklet distributed by the Office of Black Ministry, Pierre Toussaint was born in slavery on June 27, 1766 in Haiti. In 1787 his master took his family and five slaves, among them Pierre Toussaint, to New York City. When the master died shortly afterwards, Toussaint contributed to the widow's support with his earnings as a hairdresser. She provided for his manumission shortly before her own early death. Toussaint was able to buy his sister's freedom as well as that of Juliette Noel, his wife. He paid $15.12 for his aunt's grave at St. Peter's, New York City's first Catholic church. He gave the original $100 for Saint Vincent de Paul Church. Throughout his life he was a benefactor -- sometimes secretly when the recipient was white.

One biographer describes Toussaint's stance on the racial situation in America as "tranquil, contented, yet considered emancipation a blessing."[41] In the mass celebrated at his funeral the priest made no reference to Toussaint's race and little to his class: "It seemed as if his virtues as a man and a Christian had absorbed all other thoughts. A stranger would not have suspected that a black man, of his humble calling, lay in the midst of us."[42] The funeral service was attended by respectable citizens of both colors, and whereas whites did not join the funeral procession, many gathered around the grave for the committal ceremony. Toussaint had requested that none of his white friends follow the casket at the funeral of his wife, and his wish was remembered at his own funeral.[43] The graves of Toussaint's wife and adopted daughter are next to his. There is no mention of them on the gravemarker.

Mammies, Relations and Hierarchies

Many children's nurses were commemorated by grateful masters or employers, who usually disregarded the nurse's own family. The memory of the "mammy" is thus tied to the white family she served rather than to her own family or to any church, lodge, or other group to which she may have belonged. Stripped of biological and cultural ties, the black domestic's posthumous identity relies entirely on her masters or employers. This observation applies even to twentieth-century gravemarkers.

> Mamy Sarah, devoted servant of the family
> who died age sixty years.   1863[44]

> SOPHIA
> MALONE
> 1853 - 1929
> IN MEMORY
> BY THE CHILDREN
> OF MR. & MRS.
> T.J. HIGHTOWER, JR
> TO WHOM SHE WAS
> EVER FAITHFUL[45]

> LUCY HOMER
> DIED AUG. 22, 1910
> AGED 74
> DEAR MAMMY
> For Forty Years a Faithful
> Helper and Friend.

> KATIE WILSON
> BELOVED NURSE
> DIED 1927 AGE 97.[46]

Epitaphs for children's nurses provide striking examples of white employers' claims on black lives. They stress the attachment of the deceased to employers or masters and neglect to note their ties to black relatives and institutions. The frequent reference to church and lodge membership in addition to family relations on the gravemarkers erected by blacks for blacks are in marked contrast to those ordered by whites, which treat African Americans as genealogical and socio-cultural "isolates."[47]

Isolation is proclaimed for obvious political reasons. Hegemony is easily legitimized when the dominated are said to have little aptitude for building social and cultural institutions of their own. Slaves were deprived of recognized family status. By refusing slave marriages legal sanction, the lawmakers precluded all confusion over conflicting powers of patriarchal authority, such as husband over wife, parents over children, master over slave. Mary L. Duncan captures the dilemma of conflicting lines of authority when she writes about a slave child:

> But he was not his mother's child--he was his master's. She was not her own, nor her husband's--she also was her master's. And who was he?[48]

Denying slaves their biological ties robs them of their humanity. Denying the dominated ancestors and descendants dispossesses them of their place in history. Slavery was for life. Slave-holders had to impose timelessness on their slaves. Disengaged from all ties for all time as well as at any particular time, slaves were chattels, movable and therefore easily salable property. Erecting funerary monuments for them implied situating them in history. But in the epitaph a slavemaster could affirm his ownership for eternity.

Africans brought up in cultural traditions of strong kinship organization, interdependence and continual dialogue between the living and the dead members of a family encountered a radically different situation in America. In the official discourse of the slave states, formal kinship ties were denied to them, their ancestors disclaimed, their descendants not acknowledged. And yet the slaveholders' ideal coexisted with the reality of mutual accommodation of masters and slaves and with the actual persistence of African patterns of kinship and social organization.[49]

A Newport, Rhode Island, inscription bears testimony to the continuation of a West African belief which attached great importance to twins. The priority of Jem Howard's relation to the world is given to his twin brother, followed by his mother.

> In Memory of
> Jem Howard
> A Twin Brother of
> Quam & Son of
> Philis, died July
> 17th 1771 in the
> 9th Year of his Age

The epitaph of another Newport resident, buried not far from Jem Howard, does not mention blood relations but the ties to two employers.

> Here lyes the Body
> of CATO. Formerly Servt
> of M^r JOB ALMY &
> lately a Servt to M^r
> SILAS COOK of
> this TOWN. He
> died May 13, 1763
> Aged about 40 Years.

Those African Americans who happened to live in almost all-white communities may have experienced genuine isolation. The pathetically terse inscription of a woman's grave in Wayland, Massachusetts, conveys a sense of loneliness.

> Flora
> a coloured
> woman,
> AEt. 94[50]

The few words define Flora's social identity concisely by ethnicity, sex, and age. The Wayland *Vital Records* do not yield much further information; they list the death of "Flora, 'a Black woman,' May 14, 1823."[51]

A Marblehead, Massachusetts, gravestone is among the earliest memorials for African Americans:

Angelika Krüger-Kahloula

> Agnis
> Negro Woman
> Servant to
> Samuel Russel.
> July ye 12, 1718
> aged 43 years.[52]

Agnis was buried not far from her temporal owners. She died before family lots and posthumous representation of the patriarchal household became common in America.

Southern family cemeteries of later years provide neatly delineated groupings and demarcations between the generations and the races. The Blackwell Family Burying Ground in Cobb County, Georgia, furnishes an interesting example of necro-social mapping. Friends of the Blackwells, Mr. and Mrs. Oliver, were buried outside the fence, i.e. in proximity to and yet segregated from the family, in 1866 and 1886 respectively. A former slave of the Olivers, who remained with his mistress after Emancipation, is buried at their feet.[53]

What masters counted an honor did not necessarily gratify the slaves. Lewis and Milton Clarke tell the story of a man of high standing in the church who promises to remember his slave in his will in recompense for attending him well during a prolonged sickness. The slave anticipates manumission and is eager to have his hope confirmed. Eventually the master confides to him the provision he has made: when the slave dies he will receive a good casket and will be buried in the same vault as his master. Not letting on his disappointment, the slave explains that he is apprehensive about this prospect: "Why, I fraid, massa, when de debbil come take you body, he make mistake, and get mine."[54] Thus the master's claim to eternal dominance is exposed as pretentious delusion.

The Clarkes give another reason for the slave's reluctance to be buried in proximity to his master. They discern a deep and lasting psychological impact of subordination and terror:

> The slaves uniformly prefer to be buried at the greatest possible distance away from master. They are superstitious and fear that the slave-driver, having whipped so much when alive, will, somehow, be beating them when dead. I was actually as much afraid of my old master when dead, as I was when he was alive. I often dreamed of him, too, after he was dead, and thought he had actually come back again, to torment me more."[55]

West African and European world views envision the cemetery and the grave as liminal spaces where two worlds meet.[56] For those who recognize the symbolic value of the grave, contiguous burial of master and slave epitomizes utter and ultimate domination.

A master who commissioned a gravestone had to decide which of the biological and social ties the deceased had formed would be acknowledged, which would be withheld, and the order in which the ones disclosed would appear in the inscription. On a marker from Copp's Hill Burial Ground in Boston, Massachusetts, a woman is first related to her husband who is, in turn, connected with his master in a sort of hierarchical chain. It is only by implication that we can assume her to be the same master's property.

> Here lies y^e Body of
> Mary y^e
> wife of
> Ceasor Augustus
> Servant of Mr. Robert Ball
> Aged 25 years
> May 28

A Newport, Rhode Island, gravestone lists the mistress of the deceased before the mother.

Fig. 3   Flova, 1778, Princeton, Mass.

Fig. 4   Thomas, 1783, Princeton, Mass.

> In Memory of
> Phillis a Negro
> Servant to M^rs
> Ann Sabear &
> Daughter of Peg
> Collins died
> June y^e 24 1738
> Aged 18 Years.

Two markers in Princeton, Massachusetts, in memory of Flova "a Negro woman servant" and of Thomas "a Negro man servant" leave no doubt as to the relative importance of their master "the Hon^bl Moses Gill" (Figs. 3 and 4).

On a Middletown, Connecticut, marker, which mentions a slave's marital bond along with that of slavery, the master avoids any possible confusion over priorities by having his own name and claim on the deceased mentioned twice.

> In Memory of
> JENNY
> Servant to the Rev. Enoch Huntington, and wife of Mark Winthrop,
> Who died April 28, 1784
> The day of her death she was Mr. Huntington's Property.[57]

One may conjecture whether this extraordinary piece of assertive ownership was prompted by a legal dispute or whether Huntington wanted to emphasize the change from temporal to eternal ownership poor Jenny must undergo when she passed away.

Person or Property?

The question of ownership brings us back to a point raised before: since slaves were both human beings and property, their vital statistics might be classified as such or as items of bookkeeping.[58] Given the definition of slaves as property, it is hardly surprising to find passages that read like epitaphs in plantation record books. In *Our Todays and Yesterdays*, aptly named for its nostalgic approach to Southern history, Margaret Cate introduces her excerpts from one such plantation diary: "A true insight into the lives of the slaves of *Retreat* and the attitude of the mistress toward them is revealed by the record book in which Mrs. King kept the accounts of the plantation."[59] The "true insight" here translates into vital records, the "attitude" of the well-meaning mistress shows in the use of such euphemisms as "servants" or "my people" for slaves, with the possessive pronoun meant to convey identification with the "people" rather than appropriation.

Among the records quoted by Cate are the following:

- Peggy's boy child, aged 12 hours, died 18 August, 1854.
- Delia's first child died of lock jaw, 7th October 1856.
- Old Cupid, honest and true to his earthly owners, departed this life at 4 A.M., 29 January, 1857.
- My valued servant Annie died of fever, Oct. 5, 1858.
- Quamina -- most honest and true -- a faithful servant and good man, after a short illness of 24 hours, departed this life 20th March, 1860.[60]

Since babies and small children have not yet acquired social functions and status, their obituaries and epitaphs tend to be shorter than those of adults. Mrs. King's notes use evaluations of the character and life of the deceased that are very similar to those we have encountered in tomb inscriptions.

Another record, of the death of a particularly favored slave, is longer but also reads like an epitaph:

> My good and faithful servant Hannah, after years of suffering, expired on the night of the 2nd of August, 1854. For honesty, moral character, unselfishness and perfect devotion to her owners, she had not her equal. She died resigned, with firm trust in her Redeemer.[61]

Both the store of adjectives these obituaries draw upon and the themes the last two evoke are stock material of slave epitaphs. Very likely private texts such as letters and personal diaries of the time use similar themes and expressions.[62]

Other records openly acknowledge the economic loss involved in the death of a slave. The following excerpt from a Mississippi plantation diary is quoted in Phillips, *American Negro Slavery*:

> Sunday
> July 10, 1853
> Peyton is no more
> Aged 42
> Though he was a bad man in many respects
> yet he was a most excellent field
> hand, always at his
> post.
> On this place for 21 years.
> Except the measles and its sequence, the
> injury rec'd by the mule last Nov'r and its sequence,
> he has not lost 15 days' work, I verily believe, in the
> remaining 19 years. I wish we could hope for his
> eternal state.[63]

The recorder fulfills several functions. The graphic arrangement of the memorandum conveys dignity to the text: the passage reads like an obituary or an epitaph. The master expresses his concern for Peyton's spiritual welfare. While deploring his character defects, he commends his skill and willingness to work. The accounting of workdays lost serves the purpose of both character evaluation and bookkeeping. Accounting and necrology are integrated in one text.

In another diary a Texas slaveowner assesses the deceased in terms of the religion he professed and practiced rather than in terms of his capacity for work:

> Died on my farm near Franklin Tennessee May 7-1857 my Old Man Tom so well and favorable known in this community as Henderson Tom--seventy three or four years of age. He has been a regular member of the Methodist Church between forty-five and fifty years--and a more faithful and constant Christian either white or black I have seldom known. He lived like a Christian and he died like he lived in full prospect of Immortality and Eternal life.[64]

The explicit joining of black and white Christians makes ethnicity appear as a criterion of minor importance.

A grave inscription recorded by Phillips expresses hope for the deceased slave's spiritual state but also betrays the author's inclination toward bookkeeping.

> Sacred to the memory of Bill, a strictly honest and faithful servant of Cleland Belin. Bill was often intrusted with the care of Produce and Merchandize to the value of many thousand dollars, without loss or damage. He died 7th October, 1854, in the 35th year of his age, an approved member of the Black Mingo Baptist Church. Well done, thou good and faithful servant. Enter thou into Joy of thy Lord.[65]

Cleland Belin must be given credit for having Bill's name mentioned twice, thus counterbalancing the dominance of his own full name in the epitaph. The mention of large amounts of money exposes the master's wealth as well as his supreme authority over the slave, whom he entrusts with such valuables. The closing Bible quotation not only corroborates the Christian foundation of domestic servitude, but also implies a parallel between the heavenly master and the earthly one.

One of the purposes memorials serve is that of instructing the living. Since slaves in South Carolina, where the above inscription comes from, were supposed to be illiterate, the moral example of Bill was lost on most slaves passing by his tomb. Funeral sermons and gravesite addresses sometimes served the hortatory function written texts could not fulfill for the unlettered. Some addresses delivered at a slave's burial by representatives of the master class were straightforward in holding up the life of a zealous servant as a model to emulate. The following excerpt is reported from antebellum Georgia:

> He wa[s] a faithful servant and a true Christian;
> if you follow his example, and live as he lived,
> none of you need fear, when the time comes for
> you to lay here.[66]

A Providence, Rhode Island, marker makes use of the same scriptural passage as the epitaph quoted above. It also indicates the source:

> Here lies
> the Body of YARROW
> an African who after a
> Life of strict Integrity,
> He resign'd his Soul to
> GOD, April 7, 1786,
> Aged about 60 years.
> Mat. 25.23^d Well done good &
> Faithful Servant enter into the
> Joy of thy Lord
> An honest Man's the Noblest work of God.[67]

The corresponding parable, a Calvinist's delight, is about the creation of surplus value. It celebrates a servant who multiplies the money entrusted to him by his master. The lesson to be drawn is that obedience toward masters is not sufficient: a profit must be made. Capitalism and religion join hands.

Persons of Color and Respectability

An inscription from Darien City Cemetery, Georgia, honors a man who is first credited with faculties that would become a white person and then complimented on his humility.

> This
> Stone is here placed by
> J. C. TUNNO
> As a grateful expression of his
> attachment to
> GEORGE
> A free person of colour who died
> in his service in Darien
> June 6th 1822 aged 23 years.
> Having possessed the advantages of a
> decent competence, and
> a good education.
> His humble, unassuming, and correct
> deportment gained him the approbation,
> and secured him the good will
> of every liberal person under whose
> notice he chanced to fall.
> And in no heart perhaps was gratitude
> ever more strong.

With all his qualities, George was not entitled to a surname. But Tunno is careful to balance George's ability with his servility. He does not ascribe too much competence to George. This may be an adequate description of the man's talents. It may also be a concession to racist visitors to the cemetery, whose conviction of white supremacy must not be challenged. The employer's gratefulness mentioned in line four is counterbalanced by the employee's gratitude referred to in the penultimate line. All this balancing betrays an effort to eulogize a person who is considered socially inferior. It also conveys fondness for the deceased and regret.[68]

Angelika Krüger-Kahloula

Among the grave inscriptions we have looked at so far, reference to the ethnicity of the deceased takes such forms as ("Negro" or "African") "servant of," "colored," or "of color." Ethnicity may be treated as a subject in the epitaph. Color may be punned upon. A well-known example appears on the gravestone of Caesar in North Attleboro, Massachusetts (Fig. 5):

Fig. 5   Caesar, 1780, Attleboro, Mass.

Commemorating Black People

> In memory of
> CAESAR
> Here lies the best of slaves
> Now turning into dust:
> Caesar the Ethiopian craves
> A place among the just.
> His faithful soul has fled
> To realms of heavenly light,
> And by the blood that Jesus shed
> is changed from Black to White.
> Jan 15 he quitted the stage
> in the 77th year of his age.
>   1780

Attleboro historian John Daggett reports about Caesar. It seems that he was given by his mother while an infant to Lieutenant Josiah Maxcy. (This seems a little peculiar, since slavery was not abolished in Massachusetts until the adoption of its Bill of Rights in June, 1780; if Caesar's mother was still a slave, she was not in a position to decide her son's fate; if she was free, she would have been unlikely to give her child into slavery.) When Josiah Maxcy died in 1772, Caesar passed to his son, Levi Maxcy, who kept a tavern in Attleboro until the year of Caesar's death. Caesar was well known as a waiter in this tavern. Daggett goes on to say that Caesar survived his first master (Josiah) and was buried in the same yard; that a decent stone was raised over his grave by his young master (Levi); and that the only white stone in the Old North Burying Ground in Attleboro, as contrasted with the usual gray slate, was that for Maxcy's wife (presumably referring to Josiah's wife, Mary, who died in 1754, for Levi's wife was not buried there). Daggett's characterization of Caesar reads like an epitaph: "He was simple-hearted, but proved through a long life a remarkably honest and faithful servant in the family where he lived."[69]

Levi Maxcy's son and namesake, born in 1770, became a stonecarver and his father may also have followed this trade. It may be that one of them carved Caesar's stone at the time of Caesar's death or some years later. Whether the son or his father composed the epitaph, the author may have been familiar with a poem of the black Boston poet, Phillis Wheatley, published in London only a few years before, "On Being Brought from Africa to America":

> 'TWAS mercy brought me from my *Pagan* land,
> Taught my benighted soul to understand
> That there's a God, that there'a a *Saviour* too:
> Once I redemption neither sought nor knew.
> Some view our sable race with scornful eye,
> "Their colour is a diabolic die."
> Remember, *Christians, Negroes*, black as *Cain*,
> May be refin'd, and join th' angelic train.

In the old black section of the Providence, Rhode Island, North Burying Ground the markers for Charles and Lucy Haskell, a pair of large, pointed slabs decorated with the identical motif of Cantharus urns framed by drapery, are easy to make out. They are believed to have been erected by the Haskells' employer.[70]

> To
> the memory
> of
> CHARLES
> HASKELL,
> man of colour.
> A soldier of the Revolution
> He died
> the 17th of December,
> 1833,
> aged 73 years.
> He retained through life the character
> of a faithful, industrious and honest man.
> I.S. Tinley, Jr.

> In memory
> of
> Mrs. LUCY HASKELL
> Wife of
> Mr. Charles Haskell
> and Daughter of
> Pero and Phillis Brown.
> She died in May, 1812,
> aged 32 years.
> A professed disciple of Jesus Christ
> who lived in the practice of his
> precepts
> and died in hope
> of reaping the rewards of grace in
> his kingdom,
> where every *complexion* will unite
> in praising Him who has washed their
> robes
> and made them *white* in his own
> blood.

Again the pun on color occurs in the context of Christian salvation. Again blood is the medium by which redemption is achieved. To be sure, racial unity is presented in the form of a non-segregated hereafter. Placed next to the grave inscription of her husband, that of a Revolutionary soldier, however, it is hard to believe that Lucy Haskell's epitaph does not invite reflections on the social reality of this world.

The title "Mrs." that precedes the wife's name and the fact that her parents are mentioned in addition to her husband are indicators of respectability. Another Rhode Island inscription makes explicit mention of respectability:

> In Memory of
> three respectable Black
> Persons. Phillis, Rose, &
> Fanny Chace,
> who served faithfully
> in the Family of
> Samuel Chace Esqr.

Angelika Krüger-Kahloula

> The wise, the gay, the humble
> and the exalted, the beautiful
> and the deformed must all
> moulder in the same native clay.[71]

Jamie and Jay Coughtry, to whom we owe the recording of this gravestone, found that in Providence newspapers one or two slaves but no free blacks received a death notice from 1762 to 1804. Between 1804 and 1832 the deaths of less than 100 African Americans were listed, "invariably described as 'respectable' men and women 'of color'."[72] Respectability refers to moral character and to social status. Respectability and slavery are generally thought to be mutually exclusive categories; respectability and racial stigma do not appear to go well together. Persons who belong to an ethnic group that is considered inferior by the dominant group cannot lay claim to respectability unless a different or parallel set of values is applied to them. Such social camouflage will hardly deceive the individuals concerned about the actual distribution of power and attribution of respectability. As late as 1955 Hylan Lewis noted that black Americans living in the South tended to be "respect-starved".[73]

Born a Slave

A number of grave inscriptions state that the deceased was born in slavery. After Emancipation such a reference would suggest historic depth to the biography of the subject of the inscription. Slavery is evoked, along with the familiar themes of faithful service and friendship, even in twentieth-century New England, on a monument in Grove Street Cemetery, New Haven, Connecticut.

> CHARLES FENTON
> HARRIS
> BORN A SLAVE IN
> VIRGINIA,
> DIED IN NEW HAVEN
> OCTOBER 4, 1902.
> AGED 64 YEARS.
> FOR THIRTY FOUR YEARS
> A FAITHFUL SERVANT AND
> FRIEND IN THE FAMILY OF
> MORRIS TYLER AND
> OF HIS SON.[74]

A Pittsfield, Vermont, gravemarker reads:

> In memory of
> JACK YORK
> A colored person who
> died in Pittsfield, Vt.
> Aug. 29, 1874
> AE about 86 years.
> He was born a slave in Salem,
> NY. He came to Pittsfield, Vt, in
> 1820, where he was always
> ready to shake hands with all.

A metal sticker and flag placed on the grave on Memorial Day identified him as a veteran. York appears to have participated in the community life of his adopted town and state. His tombstone is situated close to the entrance of the cemetery, not really isolated but not integrated into the larger rows and clusters of graves in the central area.

In Aspen Grove Cemetery, Burlington, Iowa, a pair of markers give a compendium of the achievements of Benjamin and Catherine Sandridge:

> In memory of Benj. Sandridge, Commonly
> Known as Uncle Ben, Born a Slave in
> Virginia, Held in Bondage for 49 Years,
> Died a Free Man by the Law of His Country
> and the Grace of His God, in Iowa Nov. 7,
> 1853, Being about 53 Years of Age. Erect-
> ed by His Wife, Kitty.

> In memory of Catherine Sandridge, Commonly
> Known as "Aunt Kitty", Born a Slave. The
> Wife of Uncle Ben and with Him Made Free
> by the Payment of $1,000 to their Master.
> Both Became Members of the First Baptist
> Church of Burlington, Iowa, at its Organi-
> zation in 1849 and Were Faithful As Such to
> the End. Died Sept. 10, 1863, Being about
> 60 Years of Age. To Depart and Be With
> Christ Is Far Better.[75]

Whereas the husband's epitaph declares his freedom "by the Law of His Country and the Grace of His God", that of his wife specifies that their freedom was bought for the substantial sum of $1,000. Since it was Catherine who had the first marker put up, she must have chosen or agreed to the wording. Parts of the second epitaph may have been phrased according to her request. She thought fit to include the names by which she and her husband were known in the community, even though they were racial tags.

The inscription on a brownstone marker in East Haddam, Connecticut, which was removed from the cemetery and placed in a vault for safekeeping in 1985, reads:

> TO THE MEMORY OF JOEL A BLACK MAN BORN A SLAVE FOR LIFE
> BUT BY HIS INDUSTRY, FIDELITY, AND FAITHFULNESS OBTAINED
> HIS FREEDOM AT THE AGE OF 26 YEARS AND LIVED 14 YEARS IN
> THE FULL ENJOYMENT OF THE PRIVILEGES OF A FREE MAN.
> HE DIED JULY Y^e 12th 1802 AGED 40 YEARS [76]

The corresponding footstone is inscribed: "Joel Jackson 1802." Jonathan Twiss found out that this marker of an emancipated slave was paid for by a relative of his former master, although the man had been free for fourteen years. The account book of stonecutter Silas Brainerd of East Haddam lists the following entry under the heading "Epaphroditus Champion,

Commemorating Black People

Debtor": "1804 Nov. 29 To One pare of gravestones for Joel." The price was L2/17/0. Research on the Champion family revealed that the will of Henry Champion of Westchester, Connecticut, dated December 16, 1789, mentions that all of his former slaves, Sampson, Cate, and Joel, had been emancipated. Unless there had been some kind of financial agreement between Jackson and Epaphroditus Champion, the latter's commission of a memorial attests to his recognition of responsibility toward a former slave. If Champion bought the marker to present himself as a social benefactor, he might have had his own or his family's name included in the epitaph. The fact that Joel's first name only is mentioned on the headstone is in keeping with the image of a former slave.

The Sedgwick family plot in Stockbridge, Massachusetts, covers a large circle, with dozens of graves arranged concentrically around the obelisk and the urn-on-pedestal monuments of the parents, Theodore and Pamela Sedgwick. The site is secluded, with huge conifers and trimmed shrubs separating the Sedgwick descendants from the general population of the cemetery. Among ornate Victorian monuments and upright marble slabs with lancet or trefoil arches, a square-shouldered marker in the Sedgwick lot commemorates a former slave, whose fight for freedom ignited the judicial debate that eventually led to the abolition of slavery in Massachusetts:

> ELIZABETH FREEMANN
> known by the name of
> MUM BET
> died Dec. 28 1829
> Her supposed age
> was 85 Years.
> She was born a slave and
> remained a slave for nearly
> thirty years. She could nei-
> ther read nor write yet in
> her own sphere she had no
> superior nor equal. She nei-

> ther wasted time nor property.
> She never violated a trust, nor
> failed to perform a duty.
> In every situation of domes-
> tic trial, she was the most effi-
> cient helper and the tender
> friend: Good mother farewell.

Elizabeth Freemann left the house of her master in an argument with his wife, after receiving a blow with a heated shovel that was directed at her sister. She had lawyer Theodore Sedgwick plead her case in court. Having heard the Bill of Rights discussed by white people, she decided to claim her liberty according to the Revolutionary doctrine of freedom and equality. The jury declared her free and ordered her former master to pay her thirty shillings damages. She worked as a housekeeper and nurse for the Sedgwicks for several years before setting up house with her daughter.[77] In her will she left her daughter a black silk gown, a gift from her African father, and a gown that her African mother had worn.[78]

The epitaph, written by Catherine Maria Sedgwick, moves from slavery and humble status to "her own sphere," domestic work and care. In the domestic sphere (which is one shared by women and servants), Elizabeth Freemann practices civic virtues. She is portrayed as an admirable person, but no mention is made of her politically significant rebellion against her fate. Her rebellion brought her from a domestic, female sphere characterized by physical violence to the male world of public discourse and legal dispute. Was this distasteful to the writer of the epitaph or merely insignificant?

Commemorating Black People

Born Free...

The next epitaph does not avoid discussing politics. In fact, it carries a sweeping condemnation of slavery and a pointed comment on the current political situation, but it does so at the expense of the individual it commemorates.

> God wills us free, man wills us slaves.
> I will as God wills Gods will be done.
> Here lies the body of
> JOHN JACK.
> A native of Africa who died
> March 1773, aged about 60 years.
> Tho' born in a land of slavery,
> He was born free.
> Tho' he lived in a land of liberty,
> He lived a slave,
> Till by his honest, tho' stolen labors,
> He acquired the source of slavery
> Which gave him his freedom,
> Tho' not long before,
> Death the grand tyrant
> Gave him his final emancipation,
> And set him on a footing with kings.
> Tho' a slave to vice,
> He practised these virtues
> Without which kings are but slaves.

John Jack is buried in Old Hill Burying Ground in Concord, Massachusetts. The first record we have of him is dated 1754.[79] An inventory prepared upon the death of Benjamin Barron of Concord, a cordwainer by trade but later a farmer, lists among other items:

> One Negro servant named Jack. .... L 120:0:0
> One Negro maid named Violet, being of no vallue.

By 1761 Jack had bought his freedom and acquired four acres of plow land for L16 from Susanna Barron, his late master's daughter. He paid L6:13:4 to someone else for two more acres of land. The deed of the first purchase sets him down as "a certain Negro man called John, a Free man, now resident at said Concord, a laborer," that of the second as "Jack, a free Negro man, late servant to Benjamin Barron, deceased." The associate proprietors of the great fields in Concord name him "Jack Barron," whereas the church records mention him as "Jack, Negro."

Cobbling shoes and working for farmers, John Jack was able to buy another lot of two and a half acres on which to build his house. For more than a century after his death, this site was to house black families. In his will of December 1772 John Jack left his real and personal estate, after funeral expenses, to "Violet, a negro woman, commonly called Violet Barnes, and now dwelling with Susanna Barron." Besides his real estate he owned a cow and calf, a pair of oxen, farming tools, a Bible and psalmbook as well as seven barrels of cider-- the latter probably founding his reputation for drinking.

As Violet, who lived until 1789,[80] was only forty-five years old when Benjamin Barron died, it was more likely poor health than old age that made her "worthless" in the inventory. In 1769, when Susanna Barron inherited the homestead after her mother's death, she agreed "that she would take the negro woman belonging to the estate as her own, and that she would support her in sickness and health, she having the benefit of her labor." Whatever the terms of this settlement and the nature of Violet Barnes's relationship with John Jack were, his property went to Susanna Barron after his death, which indicated that Violet was still a slave. Concord historian George Tolman wonders how Violet's lacking qualifications for assuming an inheritance could possibly be overlooked by both John Jack and his lawyer, Daniel Bliss. As a slave she was not entitled to hold real estate. I find it difficult to believe that the lawyer ignored or disregarded this legal detail, but if there was an additional settlement between John Jack and Susanna Barron, it has not been preserved along with the will.

Whatever the legal skills of Bliss were, it is to him that John Jack owes his posthumous celebrity. As a staunch Tory, Bliss made himself quite unpopular in the early days of the Revolution. His support for the British troops was so enthusiastic that he had to flee Concord. His house on Walden Street was confiscated by the General Court and sold at auction in 1781.[81]

Bliss composed his client's epitaph and took the opportunity to point out the contradiction of America's striving for independence while denying the fundamental right of self-determination to its black population. Divine sanction of slavery is negated in the very first line of the inscription. Deeply cynical about his society and known for his sarcastic comments on his compatriots' revolutionary ambition, Bliss had no difficulty laying open the discrepancies between American rhetoric and reality. The contradictory position of pro-slavery advocates of American independence is skillfully exposed in the antithetical structure built on geographical, political, social, and moral opposites.[82]

Incidentally, American slavery and the political thinking of the Founding Fathers were closely connected, following the "logic of contradiction". Patterson points out:

> The idea of freedom and the concept of property were
> both intimately bound up with the rise of slavery,
> their very antithesis. The great innovators not only
> took slavery for granted, they insisted on its necessity
> to their way of life.[83]

This dialectic of freedom and slavery was given expression in both the form and the content of John Jack's epitaph.

According to a Concord newspaper article of 1838 a British officer copied the epitaph in 1775 and sent it back to England. It was published in a London newspaper as a satirical comment on the pretensions of the American sons of liberty. The stone has always been an object of interest.

The present monument is a facsimile of the original, the broken pieces of which had lain for several years beside the grave, when Judge Rufus Homer organized a subscription among the members of the Middlesex bar in 1830 to have a reproduction made. It was the object of a commemorative cult during the lifetime of Concord abolitionist Mary Rice, who tended the grave and planted lilies on it.

The following inscriptions are copied from two sandstone markers in First Church Cemetery, East Haddam, Connecticut:

Sacred
to the Memory of
Marget Smith
Relict of Venture
Smith who died
Dec the 17th
AD 1809, in the
79th year of her
age

Sacred to the Memory
of Venture Smith an
African tho the son of a
King he was kidnapped
& sold as a slave but by
his industry he acquired
Money to purchase his
Freedom, who Died Sept 19
1805 in ye 77th year of his
Age

There are distinct echoes of the John Jack epitaph in that of Venture Smith: in the reversal of fortune turning a prince into a slave and in his working hard to buy his freedom. Smith's misfortune is given in the passive voice; the active voice is used in the second part to give an account of his economic activity. But whereas in the Concord inscription the man's life was fitted into a rhetorical structure, this epitaph tells a story. A dramatic tale leading up to a black version of the American success story. The work ethic is applied to securing freedom, that essential idea in the American political imagination.

The Venture Smith epitaph lacks the bitterness of the John Jack inscription. Whoever the author was, his intention was different from that of Daniel Bliss when he summarized the life of John Jack. Venture Smith employed a different textual vehicle to vent his anger and frustration about the numerous injustices he had suffered. In 1798 his biography, compiled by amanuensis Elisha Niles, a former schoolteacher, was published in New London: *A narrative of the life and adventures of Venture, a native of Africa but resident above sixty years in the United States of America Related by himself.* At one point in the narrative, when he relates how, after many other hazards and misadventures, he was advised to give in to false accusations brought against him by an envious white man, his language betrays aggravation and exasperation: "Captain Hart was a *white gentleman*, and I a *poor African*, therefore it was *all right, and good enough for the black dog.*"[84]

The preface, quite in line with the grave inscription, recommends the biography to the reader for the model of "honesty, prudence, and industry" it displays. The book provides genealogical and geographical information about Venture Smith's background, such as place and approximate date of birth (Dukandarra, c. 1729), father's name (Saungu Furro) and his own name (Broteer). His original name does not appear in the epitaph.

Broteer/Venture was about eight years old when he arrived in Rhode Island. The steward on the slave ship sailing from Anamboo had paid four gallons of rum and a piece of calico for the boy and called him "Venture" because he had purchased him "with his own private venture." After several setbacks Venture Smith managed to buy his freedom at age thirty-five. Being an extraordinarily strong man--his physical strength and weight were legend--he was able to earn money by hiring himself out as a laborer and also by selling fish. Later he became an entrepreneur in several branches of business. He bought his two sons and, at age forty-four, his wife. She was pregnant then, and his purchase at that point prevented his having to buy another child later. He also bought three men and allowed them to work to reimburse him the purchase price. One of the men absconded.

Smith keeps careful account of these transactions in the biography. We learn that his son's death added a financial loss of L75 to the personal one, and that the physician's bill for attending his daughter during her lingering illness amounted to L40, almost the price he paid for her freedom eight years earlier. The casual appreciation of an individual's monetary worth is not peculiar to plantation diaries.

The Smiths moved to East Haddam, Connecticut, in 1776. When he dictated his biography, Venture Smith possessed more than 100 acres of land and three residential buildings. The 1897 edition of the *Narrative* contains an account of his funeral. The four men carrying the bier enacted a common pattern of pre-Civil-Rights ethnic choreography: "The two in front were white, proving the respect he had won, while two of his own race assisted in the rear." By the time the new edition appeared, Smith's descendants had left East Haddam, except for two who are now buried next to Venture and Marget. Solomon Smith died in 1843 at the age of sixty-six, and his daughter Eliza A. Smith Roy died in 1902, aged seventy-five. The little family congregation in the cemetery bears witness to Venture Smith's success in putting down roots in New England.

Although the markers for Smith and his wife look similar, with their soul effigy wearing the crown of righteousness on the tympanum, they were not made by the same sculptor. Our authority on East Haddam gravemarkers, Jonathan Twiss, informs us that Venture Smith's headstone was cut by John Isham, a stonecutter who lived next to the First Congregational Church. Marget Smith's headstone was cut by Silas Brainerd, who lived a quarter of a mile down the road. Twiss thinks that the epitaphs were composed by the craftsmen, who may have had a notebook with different types of epitaph for their customers to choose from.[85] If that was the case, Isham may have had a copy of John Jack's epitaph, or of one modeled after it.

A pair of dark slate markers with identical urn-and-willow motif in the cemetery behind the First Church of Jaffrey Center, New Hampshire, mark the graves of another slave who bought his freedom and that of his wife.

Sacred	Sacred
to the memory of	to the memory of
AMOS FORTUNE	VIOLATE,
who was born free in	by sale the slave of
Africa, a slave in America,	AMOS FORTUNE, by Marri
he purchased liberty	age his wife, by her
professed Christianity,	fidelity his friend and
lived reputably, &	solace, she died his widow
died hopefully,	Sept. 13, 1802,
Nov. 17, 1801	Aet 73
Aet 91	

The concise statements are reported to have been phrased by the Rev. Laban Ainsworth, friend and patron of Amos Fortune.[86]

The earliest document we possess on the life of Amos Fortune dates from 1752, when he was listed as the property of Ichabod Richardson of Woburn, Massachusetts. A manumission statement of December 30, 1763, provided for his freedom four years after that date, but it was invalid because it had not been signed. In the inventory of the Richardson estate dated August 29, 1768, a "Negro man named Amos", worth L20, is listed between a yearling heifer, valued at L1.6.8 and a Bible worth 6 shillings 8 pence. In an agreement with Richardson's widow Amos Fortune paid the last installment toward his freedom in November 1770. He was then sixty years old. Eight years later he bought Lydia Somerset for L50. She died several months afterwards and was buried in Woburn in a now unmarked grave. He bought Violet Baldwin on November 9, 1779, and married her on the tenth. Two years later they moved to Jaffrey, where Amos worked as a tanner, occasionally training apprentices, black and white. On May

Angelika Krüger-Kahloula

21, 1789, he was received into full fellowship in the First Church of Christ. On January 28, 1796, he signed as one of the twenty-two charter members of the Jaffrey Social Library.[87]

Amos Fortune's will, dated October 3, 1801, specifies the following:

> Sixthly I order my executor after my decease and after
> the decease of the Said Violet my beloved wife that
> handsome grave Stones be erected to each of us if there
> is any estate left for that purpose.

He also left money to the church and to the local school as well as to his adopted daughter. The "handsome gravestones" eventually cost $11 to make and $5 to transport and set.

Amos Fortune's epitaph also juxtaposes African freedom with American slavery, but it lacks the detached cynicism of the John Jack stone. The epitaphs of both Amos and Violet declare their slave status before moving, in a series of parallel structures, toward a climax; death at an advanced age providing the providential solution. The syntactic segments that sum up Amos Fortune's achievements consist of verbal phrases, which give the reader a sense of the activity of his life. Violet's epitaph lacks verbs except for "died" at the end. She is entirely characterized by attributive phrases, which convey an impression of her being adjunctive to Amos. This effect is reinforced by the repetition of the possessive pronoun referring back to him who bought and married her. The husband's identity is defined by economic, religious, and civic activities, the wife's, like Marget Smith's, in relation to her husband. But how elegant and touching Violet Fortune's epitaph is !

We do not know whether Amos Fortune or his wife had a part in the composition or selection of the inscriptions. What becomes apparent in a comparison of their epitaphs to that of John Jack is the professional style of the respective authors, Laban Ainsworth and Daniel Bliss. Bliss's antithetical construction betrays the lawyer. Where he leaves tensions open, Ainsworth, the minister, while using similar rhetorical devices tells Amos Fortune's life more in terms of a quest for salvation and leaves the reader with the impression of peace found. The Fortune epitaphs are neither bitter nor biting; they are compassionate. The ironies of fate are responded to and resolved by such virtues as industry, piety, and affection.

... In Africa

African origin is mentioned on two of the three gravestones for blacks that are situated on the margin of the old Wethersfield, Connecticut, burial ground. Quash Gomer's tombstone is now almost completely defaced, the front of the sandstone slab having flaked off. The two inscriptions once read:

In Memory of
FRANCOIS
who was born in Africa,
and died July 1st
1816, aged about
55 years.

In Memory of
Quash Gomer: a
Native of Angola in
Africa, brought from
there in 1748, &
died June 6th 1799
Aged 68 years.[88]

As imprecise as the designation "Angola" may have been in the late eighteenth century, it is more specific than "Africa", which is more usually found. Wethersfield historians Adams and Stiles report that Quash Gomer bought his freedom from his master in 1766 for L25.[89]

Among the epitaphs of African Americans I have read there is only one that connects Africa with negative circumstances. The following inscription, from Canandaigua, New York, subscribes to the view of Africa as a place untouched by the blessings of civilization:

> Jacob Hodges
> An African Negro
> Born in Poverty and Ignorance
> Early Tempted to Sin
> By Designing and Wicked Men
> Once Condemned as a Felon
> Converted by the Grace of God
> in Prison,
> Lived many years, a Converted
> and useful Christian,
> died Feb. 2, 1842
> About 80 years of age.[90]

Reversal of fortune is not attached to the issue of slavery in the case of Jacob Hodges. Over several pivotal stages he acts out the drama of conversion. The happy ending is found in a Christian death, a closure, yet open to the prospect of life everlasting.

In Riverside Cemetery in Farmington, Connecticut, a white marble marker commemorates one of the West Africans whose involuntary odyssey aboard the "Amistad" in 1839 captured the American imagination and led to a famous piece of litigation.[91]

> FOONE
> A native African
> who drowned while bathing
> in the centre basin Aug. 1841.
> He was one of the company
> of slaves under Cinque, on
> board the Schooner Amistad
> who asserted their rights
> & took possession of the vessel
> after having put the Captain,
> mate & others to death sparing
> their master Ruez & Montez.

Niles National Register reports on March 27, 1841: "The Amistad Negroes have left New Haven for Farmington, where they are to be placed on the farm of Mr. Williams, until able to take care of themselves." On August

21 the same paper runs the following item: "4-21. Chronicle--The Amistad Africans. One of them was drowned at Farmington, Conn. on the 7th inst." According to one writer, Foone lost his life while searching for the body of a young man who had drowned.[92] As he was an expert swimmer and had been depressed for days before the accident, it was suspected that his death was not involuntary. His host Williams wrote:

> I have no doubt that Foone drowned himself. I find that
> they entertain the belief that they will all die in
> America; they believe that when they die they will go
> immediately to Mendi and some of them think the sooner
> the better.[93]

American legends tell of newly arrived Africans who preferred suicide by drowning to slavery. Whereas Foone drowned in inland water, they usually walked into the Atlantic Ocean, the water that separated them from their families and ancestors.

The reference to Cinque in the epitaph evokes the man among the Africans who impressed New Englanders most, by his lofty appearance and self-assured manners. The inscription also makes clear that the mutinous Africans did not engage in indiscriminate massacre.

Of the fifty-three Africans who had left Havana on September 27, 1839, nine died during the sea voyage and eight in New Haven, besides Foone.[94] The jail where they were held prisoners in New Haven was opposite the old burial ground, which was not used after 1812. Those who died in jail may have been buried at the almshouse (on today's Elm Street) or in what is now called Grove Street Cemetery. In neither case is there an extant marker.

In Norwichtown, Connecticut, the following grave inscription is hard to make out because the schist marker has suffered from erosion and is covered by lichen. It is situated at the margin of the old cemetery on the edge of a hill that descended once toward a swamp but now to a bank and an auto garage in a shopping plaza.

> In Memory of
> Boston Trowtrow
> Govener of ye Affri
> can Trib he Died
> May 28 1772
> AEt 66

The inscription does not state whether Boston Trowtrow was born in Africa or America, but his surname indicates close links to African culture. Robert Farris Thompson thinks that the doubling of the name in "Trowtrow", obviously the English adaptation of an African word, suggests that the man was a West African of aristocratic birth.[95]

Trowtrow was one of the "Negro governors", here called "Governor of the African Tribe", who were elected by African Americans in New England in the late eighteenth and early nineteenth century. White historians once looked derisively upon the institution of "Negro elections" and those holding office, dismissing them as "sham officials" endowed with "mock dignity," in spite of black testimony as to the effort and seriousness invested in the position of Negro governor.[96] More recently, Joseph P. Reidy has produced a less caustic explanation of the institution. He draws parallels between black American election celebrations and African festivities and attitudes connected with political mandate. He agrees with earlier writers that by providing rituals of status reversal the elections functioned as a social safety valve among dissatisfied African Americans. But he also discerns "the structure for a viable measure of self-government" and "qualified leaders able to provide a year-round leadership" beneath the surface of social gatherings and voting procedures. Reidy also notes the recurrence of African names among the Negro Governors: Cuff, Quash, Quosh, Juba. Trowtrow may be added to the list. Evidently, African-born men were held in respect by the black community, and African names were not easily shed.[97]

Unfortunately Norwich historians appear to know nothing about Boston Trowtrow except what the inscription in the graveyard says about him. The design on the tympanum of the stone is that of an angel with large, bloated eyes, heavily outlined eyebrows and pouting mouth, the back-combed hair or wig curling over the temples. The angel's physique does not suggest that he is African. The style points to the work of an eastern Connecticut stonecutter, Josiah Manning, who lived from 1725 to 1806 and is known to have sold gravestones in Norwich in the 1770s.[98]

Black governors usually achieved local celebrity. We have the description of a former Negro governor's funeral in Hartford, Connecticut. Another Boston, also a native African, died around 1813.

> With his cocked hat and sword upon his coffin, and followed by a numerous train, he was carried into the South Congregational Church, and there Dr. Flint pronounced a sort of funeral eulogy over his remains, which were afterwards deposited in the Centre Burying Ground.[99]

The nineteenth-century historian to whom we owe this report cannot conceive of a genuine funeral eulogy held for a black person; he qualifies the speech as travesty. There are real elections for white men, parody for blacks, real eulogies for one class of people and imitations for others.

Valediction

Grave monuments, whether unique creations or standardized, may be studied for the artistic, symbolic, social, economic, psychological, or other motivations underlying their purchase or production. Working from the assumption that epitaphs provide the ultimate occasion for defining a person's social identity, we have looked at grave inscriptions of African Americans as descriptions of real, or projections of ideal, inter-ethnic relationships. Other possible features of interest, such as carved images, ornamentation and spatial organization of graves, have been largely neglected by concentrating on the epitaphs.

Given their purpose of recommending the deceased to posterity and to ancestry (or whoever is to receive them in the otherworld), grave monuments have a tendency to eulogize in both their sacred and secular messages. Disillusionment, discouragement, or dissatisfaction are conventionally considered as inappropriate sentiments to be expressed on memorials. It is therefore hardly surprising to find that African Americans have chosen different textual vehicles for voicing discontent and depression. There are few if any echoes of fugitive slave narratives in eighteenth- and nineteenth-century epitaphs.

John Jack, the subject of the epitaph that most poignantly denounces the institution of slavery, never gains contour as an individual. He appears to be acted upon by those who enslave him, by death, which gives him "his final emancipation", and by the author of the epitaph, who fits Jack's biography into a clever satirical structure. Several inscriptions inspired by that of John Jack credit their subjects with a higher degree of autonomy. Unlike his, their gravestones are set up as monuments to people rather than to political ideas.

Whereas those markers commemorate individuals who gain or regain freedom in this life, some markers set up by slaveholders for privileged slaves seem to expect the dialectic of slavery and freedom to be resolved in the world to come. Praising the slave's willingness to work without recompense, they promise compensation in the afterworld. Their vision of a democratic hereafter provides an optimistic perspective at a point that means, above all, closure: the end of life, the termination of slavery. The temporal master surrenders authority at the very moment when the heavenly master takes charge. The gravestone documents the takeover; the slavemaster exerts a last and lasting textual control over the slave's destiny.

In other epitaphs the bond of friendship is emphasized over that of slavery. Affection is substituted for respect, sentimentality for justice. Amid mutual attachment and general good feeling the slave's deprivation of individual autonomy is played down. In seeming to attach more importance to emotional ties than to legal status, epitaphs remind the reader of sentimental descriptions of slavery in pro-slavery or apologetic literature.

By stressing the ties of black individuals to masters and employers and by omitting their biological and socio-cultural relations, whites claim even the memory of blacks in a gesture of posthumous paternalism. On gravestones of African Americans slaveholders assert ownership beyond the physical lives of slaves. The memorials become monuments to racial caste and class, documents of heteronomy. Yet they may be the only evidence we have of a historically dispossessed people. Though rarely providing more than the most rudimentary vital statistics, gravemarkers are tangible records of lives. In a largely "nameless" population, they help to recover a few identities, to reconstruct a few biographies. Besides their genealogical utility, however, they matter as visible, even touchable, markers of a group of people who were made historically invisible as individuals.

Angelika Krüger-Kahloula

NOTES

1. Charles E. Stevens, *Anthony Burns: A History* (1856; reprint, New York. 1969), 167-168. More recently, David Bradley has the central character of his novel *The Chaneysville Incident* (New York, 1981, 1982) recall spending many hours in an old churchyard in Bedford, PA, in search of the gravestones of black people said to be buried there. He never finds evidence of any (174). It is not surprising that Bradley's historical reconstruction is based primarily on oral history.

2. Anybody taking a walk in the Newport, R.I., Common Burying Ground will shrug off Stevens's lament as abolitionist polemics because the entire northeast section of that cemetery is taken up by gravestones of blacks, many of them erected by slaveholders. The Newport Common Burying Ground deserves attention and detailed research that would go beyond the scope of this study, not only because of the large number of monuments involved but also because an African American, Pompe Stevens, worked in a local stonecutter's shop (probably the John Stevens shop) and signed at least two of the markers. A study of his work is being undertaken by Ann and Dickran Tashjian and we may look forward to gaining new insights into the life and work of an African American stonecutter working in a New England tradition.

    In this paper I shall be using the terms "epitaph" and "inscription" interchangeably.

3. John Brown, *Slave Life in Georgia* (1855; reprint, Savannah, 1972), 5. In a telling footnote, the editor of the 1972 edition, Alexis Chamerovzow, adds to this passage: "Brown was probably slightly older than he estimated."

4. Orlando Patterson, *Slavery and Social Death: A Comparative Study* (Cambridge, MA, 1982), 331, 332. "Honor" and"who mattered" are to be understood according to the standard of the politically, economically, and socially dominant group. We know that slaves had their own code of honor, sense of dignity, and value system.

5. Sarah B. G. Temple, *The First Hundred Years: A Short History of Cobb County, in Georgia* (Atlanta, 1935), 811.

6. Timothy Flint, *Recollections of the Last Ten Years* (1826; reprint, New York, 1968), 313.

7. Ibid.

8. In many societies, funeral expenses and gravestones are subject to social bookkeeping. Both social status and closeness of attachment of the deceased and the survivors determine the amount of resources spent on interment ceremonies and monuments. Social distinction does not end at death. Contemporary Western sensibility would find an explicit publicizing of the price paid for a memorial offensive to its idea of

piety. In the 1920s D.R. Rosevear copied several inscriptions from Nigerian grave monuments in which the cost was stated. Two of them, from Abaragba, read: "His memory. Osimaku died Jan 3 of 1923. He was love and dear to his son families and friend. This monument is made by his e-lm(?). Okpa his brother spent L30." "Her memory by the late Oti Okpa died July 14th 1927. She was a catechism girl in R.C. Mission Abaragba. Ajan Eyam her brother spent L15." D.R. Rosevear, "Cross River Tombstones," *The Nigerian Field* 41/3 (1976), 120, 121.

9. Kenneth Lindley, *Of Graves and Epitaphs* (London, 1965), 114.

10. Ibid., 114-115.

11. But is equality in assimilation the aim? Within the bounds of this paper I shall keep to the parameters set by European Americans, at the risk of participating in hegemony. In a complementary paper on African American grave decorations I hope to look at homemade markers and assemblages as evidence of a rich cultural tradition of memorializing the dead. I may have little to add, however, to the works of Robert Farris Thompson, especially chapter 2 of *Flash of the Spirit* (New York, 1983) and Elizabeth Fenn, "Honoring the Ancestors," *Southern Exposure* 13/5 (1985), 42-45. Her videotape, also entitled "Honoring the Ancestors", is available from North State Public Video, Durham, North Carolina.

12. Susan Domowitz and Renzo Mandirola, "Grave Monuments in Ivory Coast, " *African Arts* 17/4 (1984), 52.

13. Ulrich Bonnell Phillips, *Life and Labor in the Old South* (Boston, 1929), 215. Martin Luther King's memorial in Atlanta carries the same theme, taken from the burden of a famous spiritual: "Free at last, Free at last. Thank God Almighty / I'm free at last."

14. Langdon Mitchell, "The New Secession," *The Atlantic Monthly* 138 (1926), 175. As to the last line, compare Galations 3:28 and Colossians 3:11.

15. One apologist of the peculiar institution affirms: "The Slave Institution at the South increases the tendency to dignify the family. Each planter in fact is a Patriarch." (C.G. Memminger, quoted in Eugene D. Genovese, *The World the Slaveholders Made* (1969; reprint, New York, 1971), 195.)

16. Julia E. Harn, "Old Canoochee-Ogeechee Chronicles," *Georgia Historical Quarterly* 16 (1932), 150.

17. Allison Davis, Burleigh B. Gardner, Mary R. Gardner, *Deep South: A Social Anthropological Study of Caste and Class* (Chicago, 1941), 450.

18. In their discussion of the epitaph of "PHEBE / for many years a faithful domestic in the family of the late Governor Hopkins," of Providence, R.I., the authors of *Creative Survival* remind us that the white employer or slaveholder family was sustained at the expense of "the sanctity and stability of the black family." (The Rhode Island Black Heritage Society, c. 1980).

19. In the late 1930s Austin Warner attended a funeral service in New Haven held for a black servant who had worked for a single family for almost fifty years. He had also been a deacon and belonged to several lodges. "In the funeral sermon, his life was characterized by one word, 'faithfulness'--to employer, family, church, and to all his commitments." (Robert Austin Warner, *New Haven Negroes: A Social History* (1940; reprint, New York, 1969, 256).

20. Anne Sinkler Fishburne, *Belvidere: A Plantation Memory* (Columbia, S.C., 1949), 98, 107. The epitaph occurs twice in the book, on a photograph and in transcription, as if a single mention were not enough to serve the purpose of self-advertising for these heiresses of the slaveholding class.

21. Daniel Denison Slade, "The Bromfield Family," *The New England Historical and Genealogical Register*, 26:40 (1872).

22. Ibid.

23. Viator, "The Night Funeral of a Slave," *De Bow's Review*, Feb. 1856, 219.

24. Susan Dabney Smedes, *Memorials of a Southern Planter* (1887; reprint, New York, 1965), 47.

25. Ibid., 48.

26. Caroline Gilman, *Recollections of a Southern Matron* (New York, 1839), 81.

27. Ibid., 83.

28. Frederick Law Olmsted, *The Cotton Kingdom* (New York, reprint, 1953), 175. Olmsted copied several inscriptions from this cemetery. In 1843 another Northern necropolitan tourist, William Cullen Bryant, had visited it and noted the presence of nameless graves, overgrown with weeds, as well as marble, wooden, and brick monuments. William Cullen Bryant, *Letters of a Traveller* (London, 1850), 94.

29. Olmsted 1953, 176.

30. Temple 1935 (note 5), 624.

31. Bradford Kingman, *Epitaphs From Burial Hill, Plymouth, Massachusetts, From 1657 to 1892* (Brookline, MA, 1892), 175.

32. Ibid., 170.

33. Cate, Wightman 1955 (note 61), 151. We also know that Small had a strong singing voice, which "could be heard a mile". (Lydia Parrish, *Slave Songs of the Georgia Sea Islands* (New York, 1942), 191). When Cate wrote *Our Todays and Yesterdays*, she introduced Neptune Small's tale in a nostalgic mood: "The white man who has never lived among the true Southern darkies cannot know or appreciate the fine spirit of loyalty which the slave had for his master. Many stories are told of the heroism of these people in the trying days of the War Between the States, but none can rival that of Neptune Small." (1930, 155) Cate's idea of ultimate heroism on the part of the slave is that of risking his own life to secure the master's corpse, i.e. extending loyalty beyond death. Jacque, the slave mourned by Gilman (note 26), had gone even further than Neptune: he disinterred his master killed in action to bring him home to the family cemetery.

34. A. Mott supplies two prototypes in *Biographical Sketches and Interesting Anecdotes of Persons of Color* (York, 1826): "The Grateful Negro" is a servant supporting his master with his day labor wages until a lawsuit is decided in the master's favor (144); "The Faithful Negress" sacrifices her life for a white child in the St. Domingo earthquake of 1770 (145). Few slaves received lasting grave monuments in Jamaica, in contrast to the smaller Caribbean Islands, but those who did were praised in the same terms as black servants in North America. A marker in Hyde Hall estate, Trelawney, commemorates the woman in charge of the slave children of the plantation: "In memory of / Eve / An honest, obedient and / faithful Slave, by her affectionate / and grateful master, / Henry Shirley / 1800". (Frank Cundall, *Historic Jamaica* (London, 1915), 318).

35. WPA, *Delaware: A Guide to the First State* (New York, 1938), 507.

36. Ibid., 504.

37. Harry E. Davis, *A History of Freemasonry among Negroes in America* (Washington, 1946), 21.

38. Ibid., 92.

39. Ibid., 161.

40. Ibid., 20.

41. Hannah Farnham Lee, *Memoir of Pierre Toussaint, Born a Slave In St. Domingo* (Westport, Conn. n. d.), 57.

42. Ibid., 113.

43. Ibid., 114-115.

44. Old Bruton Parish Churchyard. WPA, *The Negro in Virginia* (1949; reprint, New York, 1969), 76.

45. Southview Cemetery, Atlanta, Georgia. It is interesting to note that the children's names are not given but those of the employers, with whom Sophia Malone had economic rather than affectionate ties.

46. Both Lucy Homer and Katie Wilson are buried in Grove Street Cemetery, New Haven, Conn. The later memorial is very simple and uses a nonracial occupational title.

47. I owe the term "genealogical isolate" to Orlando Patterson, 1982 (note 4), 5. Robert W. Habenstein and William M. Lamers, in *Funeral Customs the World Over* (Milwaukee, 1960), 28, mention the opposite tendency, of genealogical promotion, among the Chinese, who, in order to enhance the prestige of the deceased, sometimes add names of fictitious descendants on grave markers.

48. Mary Lundie Duncan, *America As I Found It* (London, 1852), 201.

49. Cf. Peter H. Wood, *Black Majority* (1974; New York, 1975), especially chapter V, "More Like a Negro Country". On an individual and on a community-wide level, many slaves upheld the values masters tried to rob them of. Patterson describes the reaction of African Americans to imposed isolation: "Because his kin relations were illegitimate, they were all the more cherished. Because he was considered degraded, he was all the more infused with the yearning for dignity. Because of his formal isolation and liminality, he was acutely sensitive to the realities of community." (Patterson 1982, note 4, 337).

50. I owe this reference and a rubbing of the marker to Judith Cataldo. Raymond L. Brown provides a transcription of a monument dated 1796 for Sunderland Point, Lancaster, England. It emphasizes the solitude of a dislocated African who was buried there sixty years before the memorial was erected. The long inscription starts with the following words: "RESPECT THIS LONELY GRAVE / Here lies / Poor SAMBO / A faithful NEGRO / Who / (Attending his Master from the West Indies) / DIED on his Arrival at SUNDERLAND / ..." (*A Book of Epitaphs* (New York, 1967), 76). In the poem printed below, the first quatrain deplores the black alien's loneliness, the harsh coastal climate of Lancastershire providing imagery that correlates with the man's social estrangement. The second stanza then includes him in the (natural) cycle of the seasons, the third in the (supernatural) reunion of the souls, when approbation is based "Not on Man's COLOR but his "WORTH OF HEART."

51. *Vital Records of Wayland Massachusetts. To the Year 1850.* (Boston, 1910).

52. John Francis Marion, *Famous and Curious Cemeteries* (New York, 1977), 116. One of the motivations underlying the demand for posthumous togetherness was probably growing family sentiment with stronger marital and paternal/filial emotional attachment and weakened parochial ties. In 1797 the New Burying Ground in New Haven, Conn., was the first American cemetery to lay out family lots. (Ellen Strong Bartlett, *Historical Sketches of New Haven* (New Haven, 1897), 42).

53. Temple 1935 (note 5), 809.

54. Lewis and Milton Clarke, *Narratives of the Sufferings of Lewis and Milton Clarke* (Boston, 1846), 119.

55. Ibid.

56. European and Euro-American readers who do not recognize this concept as part of their cultural heritage are referred to "Cinderella" or to "Dynasty". In the latter TV program it is not unusual for an Anglo-American capitalist of the late 1980s to talk to his mother's gravestone.

57. William C. Nell, *The Colored Patriots of the American Revolution* (Boston, 1855), 144. In spite of detailed instructions from William Hosley of the Hartford Atheneum and the technical skills of two Middletown firefighters, I have not been able to locate this marker and am tempted to think that it is lost.

58. One dismal consequence of the socially constructed category of chattel, both person and property, was for the slaves the ever-present menace of being killed by their masters or other white persons, who, depending on the circumstances, might be acquitted of homicide charges or be fined only. A fine was considered appropriate punishment for an offense against property. A master whose slave was killed by another white person could recover civil damages. (David L. Child, *The Despotism of Freedom* (Boston, 1833), 31). The question of how much a slave's life was worth was the subject of numerous lawsuits. At times the funeral charges were part of the deal. In an 1836 Louisiana case a slave had died nine or ten months after changing masters. The purchaser had paid $700 for the woman and spent more than $150 on nursing and medical attention. In a supplemental petition he claimed $100 for funeral charges. The court decreed the return of the sales price with interest and $17 for funeral expenses. (*Saul v. Magee*: Helen T. Catterall, *Judicial Cases Concerning American Slavery and the Negro*, 5 vols. (Washington, 1926-1937), 3:511.

59. Margaret Davis Cate, *Our Todays and Yesterdays: A Story of Brunswick and the Coastal Islands* (Brunswick, Georgia, 1930), 127.

60. Ibid., 128.

61. Ibid. The 1955 edition of Margaret Cate, Orrin Sage Wightman, *Early Days of Coastal Georgia* (New York and St. Simon's Island), 75, gives the 3rd of August as date of death.

62. To my knowledge we have studies of death news only in diaries and letters of Anglo-Americans, e.g. Lewis O. Saum, *The Popular Mood of Pre-Civil War America* (Westport, Conn., 1980), chapter 4, "Death". Karen Cox, Betse Whilden, "Old Time Burials,"*Foxfire* 6/1 (1972), 8-25, use reproductions of letters as illustrations.

63. Ulrich Bonnell Phillips, *American Negro Slavery* (New York, 1918), 292.

64. Chase C. Mooney, *Slavery in Tennessee* (Bloomington, 1957), 90-91.

65. Phillips 1929 (note 13), 215.

66. Viator 1856 (note 23), 220.

67. Jamie Coughtry, Jay Coughtry, "Black Pauper Burial Records: Providence, Rhode Island, 1777-1831," *Rhode Island History* 44/4 (1985), 113. I should like to thank Robert P. Emlen of the Nicholas Brown Foundation for this reference and for that in note 71. The last line is from Alexander Pope's "Essay on Man" ("Moral Essays", Epistle IV, line 248).

68. Perhaps newspapers could afford to be more outspoken about the achievements of African Americans. To be sure, they could be challenged by letters to the editor, subscriptions cancelled, presses smashed, printers lynched, but since they catered to a more educated public, they may have put forth statements that, if chiselled in stone, would have invited vandalism. A study matching epitaphs with obituaries could determine the influence of the medium on the message. Sidney Kaplan, *The Black Presence in the Era of the American Revolution: 1770-1780* (Washington, 1973), item 64, has a facsimile of Tom Fuller's obituary. After identifying him by first name and as property of Mrs. Elizabeth Cox of Alexandria, the author of the obituary praises Tom's faculties and ends with the assertion: "Had his opportunities of improvement been equal to those of thousands of his fellow-men, neither the Royal Society of London, the Academy of Sciences at Paris, nor even a NEWTON himself, need have been ashamed to acknowledge him a Brother in Science."

69. John Daggett, *History of Attleborough* (Boston, 1894), 727.

70. Andrew Kull, *New England Cemeteries: A Collector's Guide* (Brattleboro, Vt., 1975), 198.

71. Coughtry, Coughtry, 1985 (note 67), 111.

72. George Champlin Mason, *Reminiscences of Newport* (Newport, 1884), 107.

73. Hylan Lewis, *Blackways of Kent* (Chapel Hill, 1955), 221. Another Newport marker provides a characterization written by a white man which is not condescending:

> In
> Memory
> Of
> DUTCHESS QUAMINO
> A free black,
> of distinguished excellence:
> Intelligent, industrious
> affectionate, honest
> and of
> Exemplary Piety:
> who deceased
> June 29, 1804, aged 65 years
> "Blest thy slumbers in this house of clay
> And bright thy rising to eternal day."

William E. Channing is supposed to be the author of this epitaph. (Robert S. Franklin, "Newport Cemeteries," *Special Bulletin of the Newport Historical Society* 10 (December 1913), 29) Duchess Quamino was famous for her cakes. Once a year she entertained the three families she had served before emancipation. (Lorenzo J. Greene, *The Negro in Colonial New England, 1620-1776* (New York, 1942), 307.)

74. This inscription, like those of Katie Wilson and Lucy Homer, were pointed out to me by the superintendent of Grove Street Cemetery, New Haven, William M. Cameron Jr., an inexhaustable source of information and a very kind friend. He calls the plant growing behind the Tyler/Harris monument "African tiger lily". It very much resembles plants that I have seen in most of the black cemeteries I have visited in the Eastern United States. Since I found only three such plants in Grove Street Cemetery, I doubt whether its presence at Fenton Harris's grave is entirely fortuitous. Morris Tyler, great-grandson of the employer mentioned in the Harris epitaph, was so kind as to share his childhood memories of Fenton Harris with me.

75. Charles L. Wallis, *Stories on Stone: A Book of American Epitaphs* (New York, 1954), 71-72.

76. I should like to express my sincere thanks to Beth Rich, the AGS archivist, who made this material available to me, and to Jonathan P. Twiss, who shared his research results on Joel Jackson and Venture Smith with me.

77. Rayford W. Logan, Michael R. Winston, *Dictionary of American Negro Biography* (New York, 1982), 244.

78. Sidney Kaplan 1973 (note 68), 217.

79. Unless otherwise noted, the information about John Jack and his stone is taken from George Tolman, *John Jack, The Slave, and Daniel Bliss, The Tory* (Concord, c. 1902), 16-18.

80. *Concord, Massachusetts: Births, Marriages, and Deaths, 1635-1850* (Concord, 1894), 419.

81. Ruth R. Wheeler, *Concord: Climate for Freedom* (Concord, 1967), 109; Robert Gross, *The Minutemen and Their World* (New York, 1976), 168.

82. Wheeler, op. cit., 86; Gross, op. cit., 97.

83. Patterson 1982 (note 4), VIII, IX. The peculiarities of the rhetorical construction of the John Jack epitaph make Tolman assume that Bliss wrote the original in Latin. This need not be the case, but the balanced structure, reminiscent of Juvenal and Martial, certainly betrays familiarity with Latin literature. This is no surprise in an eighteenth-century lawyer.

84. Venture Smith, *A narrative...* (New London, 1798), 30. The facts cited in the next four paragraphs of the text are taken from the *Narrative*, IV, 5, 13, 27, 26, 28, 36.

85. Personal communication from Jonathan P. Twiss, Dec. 14, 1987.

86. F. Alexander Magoun, *Amos Fortune's Choice: The Story of a Negro Slave's Struggle for Self-Fulfillment* (Freeport, Maine, 1964), 1, 94, 115, 134, 146. In 1955, February 20 was proclaimed Amos Fortune Day in New Hampshire. Except as noted, the facts in the next two paragraphs are taken from Magoun, 302, 223-4, 236.

87. Sidney Kaplan 1973 (note 68), 226.

88. Edward Sweetser Tillotson, *Wethersfield Inscriptions* (Hartford, Conn., 1899), 59.

89. Sherman W. Adams, Henry R. Stiles, *The History of Ancient Wethersfield* (Wethersfield, Conn., 1904, reprint 1974), 700.

90. Wallis 1954 (note 75), 72-73.

91. On August 26, 1839, a suspicious schooner, which had been sighted off the Long Island coast for two days, was seized by the United States brig *Washington*. The *Amistad* was not flying a flag at the time and was controlled by forty-four Africans, but

Commemorating Black People

there turned out to be two white men on board, Cubans José Ruiz and Pedro Montez, who asserted ownership of the blacks as their slaves. They had left Havana for another Cuban port on June 28, the slaves had mutinied and killed the captain and the cook. The other crew members escaped in a boat. Ruiz and Montez were spared but ordered to navigate the ship to Africa. Steering east in the daytime but northwest at night they managed to sail toward the North American coast. The mutineers were taken to New London, then to New Haven and later to Hartford to be tried for murder and piracy. Ruiz and Montez, however, preferred the slaves to be returned to them rather than having them executed and they filed corresponding claims on September 18. In the meantime, antislavery leaders had organized a defense committee for the mutineers. As the Africans spoke neither English nor Spanish, they could not be questioned until Yale Professor of Theology J.W. Gibbs found a sailor from Sierra Leone who then served as an interpreter. The defense counsel, including John Quincy Adams, learned that the West Africans had been captured and sold into slavery only a few months before. As the slave trade was prohibited by Spanish law, their slave status in Cuba had been illegal and could not be maintained in the United States. A New Haven court in January 1840 ruled that the Africans were free and that they should be transported back to Africa in accordance with an 1819 statute. The ensuing legal battle, complicated by diplomatic discord with Spain, took the "Amistad Affair" to the United States Supreme Court, which declared the captives free on March 9, 1842. Since no provision was made for their passage back to Africa, funds had to be raised among supporters of the antislavery cause before the Africans were shipped back to their home country later that year.

92. Ellen Strong Bartlett, "The Amistad Captives," *The New England Magazine* N.S. 22/1 (1900), 87.

93. Mary Cable, *Black Odyssey: The Case of the Slave Ship Amistad* (New York, 1971), 123.

94. Bernard Christian Steiner, "History of Slavery in Connecticut," (1893), in *Slavery in the States* (1969), 68.

95. Lecture "From West Africa to the Black Americas: The Black Atlantic Visual Tradition", Spring semester 1986, Yale University. Lecture note for March 25, 1986: "Trow-trow= toro-toro by analogy with Fra-Fra - fara-fara. Doubling the name equals nobility of descent..."

96. George S. Porter, *Inscriptions From Gravestones on the Old Burying Ground, Norwich Town, Connecticut* (Norwich, 1933), 6; Ebenezer D. Bassett, quoted in Orville H. Platt, "Negro Governors," *Papers of the New Haven Colony Historical Society* 6 (1900), 331.

97. Joseph P. Reidy, "Negro Election Day and Black Community Life in New England, 1750-1860," *Marxist Perspectives*, Fall 1978, 112; 108. A black man named Leb Quy from Norwich served as a Continental soldier for three years and was one of the town's quota during the War of Independence in 1780 and 1781. (Frances M. Caulkins, *History of Norwich, Connecticut* (Norwich, 1874), 331).

98. Ernest Caulfield, "Connecticut Gravestones VIII: Josiah Manning (1725-1806)," *The Connecticut Historical Society Bulletin* 27/3 (1962), 76-84; Ibid., "Connecticut Gravestones XV: Three Manning Imitators," *The Connecticut Historical Society Bulletin* 43/1 (1978), 1-16. Caulfield points out the similarities between Manning's work and that of John Walden II. A distinctive feature that helps to differentiate the work of the two is the form of the soul effigy: whereas the Manning faces are oval, those of Walden are perfect circles. (1978, 12) The Trowtrow marker features an oval face. I want to thank Alfred M. Fredette for drawing my attention to this point.

99. Scaeba (I.E. Stuart), *Hartford in the Olden Time: Its First Thirty Years* (Hartford, 1853), 40.

Fig. 1 Typical concrete "dove and cross" style marker crafted by Renial Culbreth. The inscription is made by pressing commercially-produced letters into the wet concrete. Irene McLaurin, 1968, Mt. Zion AMEZ Churchyard, Cumberland County.

AFRO-AMERICAN GRAVEMARKERS IN NORTH CAROLINA

M. Ruth Little

Sleep on Mother
We Love You But God
Loves U Best

This epitaph for an eastern North Carolina black woman who died in 1968, made with store-bought letters pressed into wet concrete by a local blacksmith, expresses the essential qualities of the gravemarkers that are the subject of this study. The marker is made of inexpensive materials by a local black craftsman, and it is emotionally direct in both its words and its pictorial symbols, a cross, dove and vase of flowers (Fig. 1).

The Afro-American tradition, as exemplified largely in twentieth-century graves, was one of the North Carolina traditions of marker design investigated by the author from 1980 to 1982 (the others being the English, Scottish and German). Four basic types of black markers--the grave mound, the head and foot marker, the grave enclosure and the grave sculpture--were recorded during intensive fieldwork in four of the total one hundred counties in the state. These four counties, New Hanover, Cumberland, Davidson and Lincoln, represent a geographic and ethnic cross-section. North Carolina had a substantial slave population during the antebellum period, and two of the counties, New Hanover and Cumberland, are in the eastern region where the slave population was concentrated.

The author recorded thirty-two black graveyards in Cumberland County, twelve in New Hanover county and seven in Davidson County (see map). Also recorded were selected black folk markers in the eastern and piedmont regions of the state. Most of the recorded graveyards are church-yards belonging to the AME Zion and Baptist denominations in

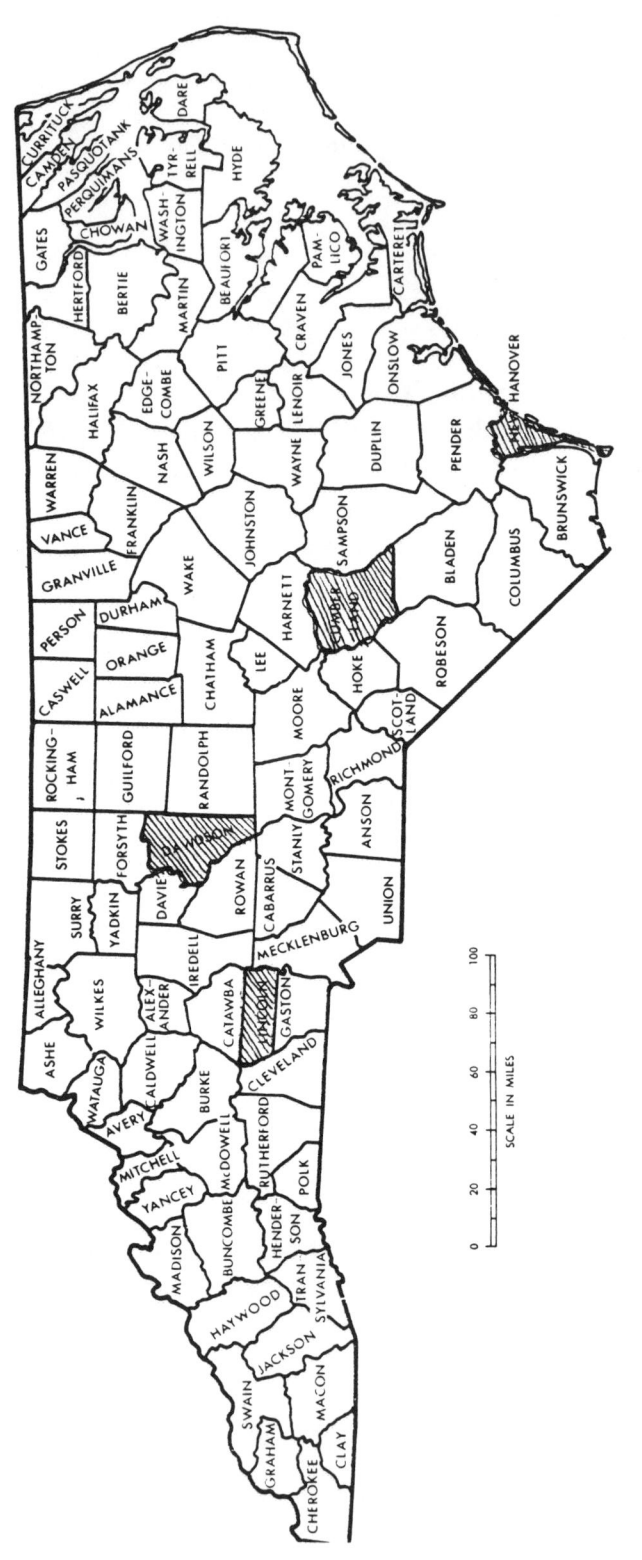

Map of North Carolina. Hatched counties were the sites of comprehensive inventories of graveyards made by the author for the North Carolina Gravemarker Survey. Approximately fifty black graveyards were recorded in these four counties and serve as the database for this study.

the east and to the Baptist denomination in the piedmont, and most of those studied date back no earlier than 1900. The preponderance of church-yards is explained by the survey methodology, which was to locate graveyards on United States Geological Survey maps and existing cemetery inventories. Most small family and community graveyards do not show up in these sources. This is an intensive study and sampling of a comparatively small area. Little has been written on the general subject, and the books and articles which have been published are not widely available. Examples are cited in the footnotes.[1]

When analyzing North Carolina gravemarkers as a category of artifacts important to the study of material culture, two primary dichotomies emerge: the folk/popular and the black/white. These occur in many permutations in the recorded graveyards. In all four counties the rural dispersal of the population and the generally agricultural economy have preserved the isolated folk nature of many black communities. There is more similarity between individual markers for blacks and whites than there is between the overall design of black graveyards and white graveyards. Nevertheless, there are fundamental visual distinctions in black and white grave traditions in North Carolina.[2]

In general, the style, material and craftmanship of gravemarkers for blacks relate to the socio-economic status of the family, just as they do in gravemarkers for whites. In large black urban cemeteries where wealthy black families are buried, the professionally carved marble monument is the aesthetic norm. But in rural community graveyards the markers fall into the folk category. The chief difference at the lower end of the socio-economic spectrum between gravemarkers for blacks and whites is that black craftsmen are less guided by popular and academic gravestone traditions and are more original.

M. Ruth Little

The most striking difference between graveyards for blacks and those for whites is in overall design. With the exception of large urban public cemeteries for blacks, the layout of black family and church graveyards has distinct, easily distinguishable characteristics. These yards are usually in wooded areas where high grass, undergrowth and trees prevent the observer from gaining a clear vista of the entire graveyard. As in white graveyards, individual graves are generally oriented east-west, i.e., head to west, feet to east. However, black graves are not aligned parallel with each other or in rows as are white graves. Families are loosely grouped, but the placement of individual graves within the family grouping has no established order, so that the rhythm of the overall design is irregular and strongly individualistic. In eastern North Carolina, where grave plots are often enclosed by fences, the unit of enclosure in white graveyards is the family plot; in black graveyards it is the individual grave.

A second striking distinction between white and black graveyards is in the design of the individual markers. A majority of markers in rural black graveyards are homemade. In materials and symbolism a characteristic set of aesthetic ideals is in evidence. The materials are ephemeral: either found objects such as shells and bric-a-brac; commercial metal and plastic items intended for functional household use; concrete; or perishable materials such as sculpted earth and wood. Shells and objects used by the deceased, such as lamps, bowls, vases and mirrors, may have more than decorative function when serving as grave ornaments. Research by American folklorists has shown that the practice of placing broken household objects on graves has been explained by blacks themselves as a means of appeasing the spirit of the deceased and of preventing the spirit from returning to the home.[3]

Unfortunately, only a handful of pre-twentieth-century black folk gravemarkers were found. Most eighteenth- and nineteenth-century folk gravemarkers for whites are made of stone, which has a relatively high rate of survival. If the pre-twentieth-century black folk markers were created from the same type of ephemeral materials that are being used in the twentieth century, it is obvious why they have not survived. Although many reputed slave graveyards survive in North Carolina, the markers in those seen by the author are either uninscribed fieldstones or, rarely, a professionally carved marble headstone. Many of these slave yards have no visible markers at all, although archaeological research may uncover evidence that markers once existed.

Only one of thirty-two black graveyards recorded in Cumberland County, in the Coastal Plain, is known to be a slave graveyard: the Evans Slave Graveyard adjacent to the Evans Family Graveyard on the Cape Fear River. It contains the only two black markers with antebellum dates recorded by the author. The markers are small, plain, marble headstones with these inscriptions:

> My own good LUCY
> died 1856
> aged 36 yrs
>
> UNCLE HARRY
> died 1856
> aged ___ yrs
>
> Mark the perfect
> man.

These two stones contribute little to understanding slave gravemarker traditions, for they reflect the aesthetic of Lucy's and Harry's white masters rather than of the slaves themselves. It is possible that even in death slaves were not free to express themselves and mark graves in their own way. This is an open question which the tools of oral history and historical archaeology may someday answer.

M. Ruth Little

All the other gravemarkers found by the author in black family, community, church and public graveyards date after the Civil War, and, with only a handful of exceptions, after 1900. Although slave graveyards certainly existed throughout the areas of plantation economy in North Carolina, depressions are all that are visible in most of them. However, it is possible that some slave burial customs can be inferred from twentieth-century black graveyards, for death traditions are durable, and it is likely that there are eighteenth- and nineteenth-century precedents for the four types of black gravemarkers made in this century: grave mounds, head and foot markers, grave enclosures and grave sculpture.

Grave Mounds

The dirt grave mound, the minimal marker, is a venerable black tradition often found in combination with other types of markers. Because of sinking and erosion, the grave mound must be reworked periodically if the shape is to be maintained. If this reworking rarely occurs, it may be because of belief rather than neglect. During the author's inspection of the Burns family graveyard in east Cumberland County, Miss Lisa, an eighty-year-old member of the family, asked a relative about a row of four fresh grave mounds. She was told that one was a new grave and that the other three were reworked when the new grave was dug. Miss Lisa exclaimed, "It's bad luck to rework a grave. Supposed to just let 'em sink on down."[4]

Dirt grave mounds decorated with sea shells, common in the Coastal Plain, are found in black rural graveyards less frequently than in white rural graveyards. The practice of decorating graves with shells may occur less frequently among blacks, but a reason for the disparity may be the generally inferior maintenance of black graveyards, allowing shells to be scattered and hidden by undergrowth. Shell grave mounds are present in two black New Hanover County graveyards, Hank's Chapel AME Churchyard and the Flemington Cemetery.

At Swans Creek Baptist Church and Willis Creek Church in Cumberland County there are groups of grave mounds that are covered with concrete stucco. Most of these mounds have headstones and footstones that carry the inscriptions, but an interesting variation is the inscription for M.B. McNair (d. 1959), which is hand-lettered in the side of the concrete-covered mound.

In the 1960s a flat concrete slab, installed by the funeral home on top of the concrete grave vault, came into widespread use in eastern North Carolina black graveyards, and these slabs continue to be popular there. No examples were found in the white graveyards. The inscription is on a small tablet, usually of marble or bronze, embedded in the head end of the slab. The funeral home often places a small plaque identifying itself at the foot end of the slab. Sometimes a decorative plaster or bronze relief sculpture, such as Christ kneeling at the Mount of Olives or a pair of praying hands or a feather, is embedded in the center or lower end of the slab. Most slabs have a smooth finish covered with white paint, but they occasionally have a rusticated finish and sometimes a covering of reflective silver paint (Fig. 2). In West Africa the grave symbolized the bottom of a river bed where the soul rested, and mirrors on the grave created the impression of reflective water.[5]

Head and Foot Markers

The single most common type of black gravemarker is the concrete headstone, usually hand-crafted rather than ordered from one of the large suppliers of the concrete headstones found in white graveyards. The only evidence of mass production of concrete markers within a black community is in New Hanover County. During the 1960s the Shaw Funeral Home, the oldest black undertaking company in operation in Wilmington, made concrete headstones with a rectangular recess fitted with a cardboard plaque containing a stamped inscription.[6] The company abandoned this short-lived experiment in the late 1960s, but many of its products are standing in the county's black graveyards.

In both New Hanover and Cumberland counties there is ample evidence that local black craftsmen made concrete headstones. The vast majority of these are plain, but occasionally they are self-conscious imitations of professionally manufactured markers or creative improvisations. The New Hanover craftsmen did not sign their work, and they remain anonymous, but oral history may uncover some of their identities.

Fig. 2   Silver-painted concrete grave slab. The funeral home's identifying tablet and a relief sculpture of a feather are embedded in the concrete. Frances G. Gainey, 1980, Mt. Zion AMEZ Churchyard, Cumberland County.

The author has identified two men in Cumberland County who engaged in sidelines of making coffins, digging graves and then the fashioning of head and foot markers. They are Renial Culbreth and Issiah McEachin.

Renial Culbreth

Nine of the black graveyards in Cumberland County contain markers made by Renial Culbreth, a blacksmith who made gravestones as a sideline, through individual commission, from the 1940s to the 1960s (Fig. 3). Culbreth was born near Vander in east Cumberland County on May 28, 1892. He was a blacksmith in Vander and later in Roseboro, in adjacent Sampson County. Before the advent of professional undertakers in the black community, which probably occurred after World War II, he made wooden coffins and carried bodies to the graveyard in his horse-drawn wagon. In later years he cast concrete gravestones, working out of his blacksmith shop in Roseboro and, in his last years, in a shed behind his house in the 600 block of West Railroad Street, Roseboro. He died January 30, 1974.[7]

Approximately twenty of Culbreth's markers within a twenty-mile radius of Vander were located and recorded by the author. According to Culbreth's family, his work may also be found in adjacent Bladen and Sampson Counties. He used a repertoire of four headstone shapes, corresponding to the four wooden molds he fashioned: the scroll, the tablet, the dove and cross, and the double headstone with urn. Concrete was poured into the wooden mold to produce the basic form. Then commercially produced letters and numbers were pressed into the wet concrete to incise the inscription, and small wooden press molds and scraps of metal were pressed in for relief decoration. The last step was to paint the entire marker white. Most of the paint has worn off Culbreth's markers.

Fig. 3 Renial Culbreth (1892-1974), blacksmith, undertaker and maker of coffins and gravemarkers. At home in Roseboro, Sampson County, in the 1960s.

Fig. 4 Typical "scroll style" marker crafted in concrete by Renial Culbreth. Clinnie M. Owens (d. 1966) First Baptist Church, Stedman vicinity, Sampson County.

Afro-American Gravemarkers in North Carolina

The headstone of Clinnie M. Owens (d. 1966), at the First Baptist Church, Stedman vicinity, is typical of Culbreth's scroll design (Fig. 4). It is a thick concrete headstone on a concrete base, with a segmental-arched top. Culbreth cast strips of wooden molding into the top of the front surface to give the effect of a molded pediment. An arched recessed panel beneath the pediment contains the name of the deceased, and birth and death dates are at the bottom, below a large scroll inscribed, "THE LORD IS MY SHEPHERD." Abstract curvilinear motifs decorate the top corners. The molds for the scroll and the corner decoration were apparently metal strips bent to the desired shapes.

Fig. 5 Typical "tablet-style" marker crafted in concrete by Renial Culbreth. Dixon McLaurin, 1949, Mt. Zion AMEZ Churchyard, Cumberland County.

M. Ruth Little

Culbreth's second basic design resembles a tablet resting on a stand. The headstone of Dixon McLaurin (d. 1949), at Mt. Zion AMEZ Churchyard, is typical (Fig. 5). The inscription, with curvilinear floral designs beneath it, is within a rectangular frame supported at a forty-five degree angle on a concrete base. The somewhat unusual shape is probably imitative of a recognition plaque set on a display stand.

The third basic design, the dove and cross, is a large segmental-arched headstone on a concrete base. Its decoration and symbolism are complex. On an example at Mt. Zion Churchyard are a large dove in flight with rays of light beaming toward it, a cross and a vase of flowers (Fig. 1). Fitted in among these decorative symbols is the inscription:

IRENE McLAURIN
B 1895
D June 14 1968

SLEEP ON MOTHER
WE LOVE YOU BUT GOD
LOVES U BEST

Another example of Culbreth's dove- and cross-design is the headstone for Charlie Fuller at Lock's Creek AME Zion Church, with the epitaph:

HE IS GONE
SLEEP ON
TAKE YOUR
REST

Culbreth's fourth design, an urn flanked by two headstones, comes from popular patternbooks supplied by monument firms in Elberton, Georgia.[8] The only example of this design found by the author is for John and Laura Geddie (d. 1941 and 1942) in the Kelly-McLaurin Graveyard (Fig. 6). Each flanking headstone is inscribed and decorated with abstract curvilinear designs in the corners. A central cross is inscribed:

DEATH IS THE CROWN OF LIFE

    FATHER
    AND
    MOTHER

The basic shapes used by Renial Culbreth correspond closely to popular commercial marble monument design. His originality emerges in the decoration which he pressed into the wet concrete with his hand-crafted molds of doves, scrolls, vases of flowers, crosses and floral ornament. Although he probably drew much of his imagery from commercial marble monuments, he simplified it and used it in novel combinations meaningful to his own community--the AMEZ congregations of Cumberland and Sampson Counties. As part of a tradition of homemade concrete gravemarker production in black settlements of eastern North Carolina, Culbreth's work easily fits the definition of folk art as art produced outside the mainstream of rapidly changing fashions.

Fig. 6 An urn and cross flanked by two inscribed markers, crafted in concrete by Renial Culbreth. John and Laura Geddie, 1941, 1942, Kelly-McLaurin Graveyard, Cumberland County.

M. Ruth Little

Issiah McEachin

Issiah McEachin, the second black folk gravemarker artist identified by the author, lives and works in Cumberland County. Ten of his markers stand within a fifteen-mile radius of his home in Eastover, a small community east of Fayetteville.[9] McEachin (pronounced McAhern) was born on June 15, 1922, near Red Springs in Robeson County, south of Cumberland. Following World War II, he trained as a brick mason with Player Construction Company in Fayetteville. He is now self-employed. McEachin is a jovial, middle-aged man who lives with his wife in a one-story frame house at 2596 Haywood Road, a sandy dirt road surrounded by tobacco and corn fields (Fig. 7). His ingenuity and creativity are evident in the attractive semicircular brick steps he added to his front porch and in the Victorian brackets and spindlework he recycled and installed on his porch in an unorthodox, upside-down position.

Fig. 7 Issiah McEachin (1922-), gravedigger and gravestone maker, at home in Eastover, Cumberland County, 1982.

McEachin began making gravestones about 1970 as a result of another part-time occupation -- grave digging. After digging inadvertently into inadequately marked existing graves, he recognized the need for good, inexpensive gravemarkers in his community. He has made about eighteen markers; for each he charged about fifty dollars and worked a total of about two and one-half hours. Like Culbreth, he builds his own wooden molds and uses commercially produced metal letters and numbers for incising the inscriptions. The only decorations on his stones are children's glass playing marbles, which he presses into the wet concrete to form borders. The idea of using marbles occured to him as a substitute for the shiny quality of granite, which he wanted to duplicate but could not achieve with the rough surfaces of concrete. He casts the markers on a framework of steel rods, like those used in concrete footings, and leaves portions exposed at the base to bury in the ground when the marker is put in place. McEachin notes proudly that the marbles are impossible to chisel out because he buries them in the concrete by about three-fourths of their diameter. McEachin had one marker on order at the time of his interview with the author. His dream for the future is to make brick gravemarkers with inscriptions fashioned of metal letters attached to the brick or cast into a concrete panel set into the brick. Meanwhile, McEachin's "marble markers" have a whimsy that distinguishes them from other homemade and professional markers in local cemeteries. The headstone of Ernest L. Barkin, at Flea Hill Church, is typical of his work (Fig. 8). The inscripton reads:

```
ERNEST L.
BARKIN
BORN JULY 1
1951
DIE APRIL 4
1970
```

Fig. 8 Concrete marker decorated with glass marbles, typical of whimsical markers made by Issiah McEachin. Ernest L. Barkin, 1970, Flea Hill Church, Cumberland County.

Multi-colored marbles are pressed into the sides and around the top of the Barkin marker to form a triangular pediment. The footstone is a concrete plaque inscribed with the name of the deceased and decorated with a border of imbedded marbles. All of McEachin's markers have the same basic shape, and all but one are decorated with multi-colored marbles. The exception, the headstone for Edith Whitted (d. 1971) at Mt. Zion Church, has borders of marbles that are all green.

Like the markers of Renial Culbreth, McEachin's markers are concrete copies of popular grave monuments, personalized with his unique decoration. The use of children's marbles is apparently original, and his contribution to the tradition of creative recycling of materials to decorate gravemarkers gives McEachin a place in black folk art.

Anonymous Craftsmen

Several other groups of artistic concrete markers exist in black graveyards in Cumberland and New Hanover Counties, but their makers remain anonymous. Some used fraternal symbols, which are relatively common on black gravemarkers. At Spring Hill Church near Hope Mills is a plain concrete headstone for D.D. Dixon (d. 1907) with the traditional Masonic compass and square cast into the top, using the actual objects as press molds. One craftsman working in the 1930s and 1940s in south Cumberland County used a symbol which may signify a fraternal organization such as the Knights of Pythias or the Eastern Star (the women's division of the Masonic Order). His markers are cast concrete headstones with rounded tops; they are set on concrete bases, and the inscriptions are hand-lettered in the wet concrete. A press mold, probably fabricated from pieces of metal, was used to inscribe the symbols. The headstone of Jannie McAlister, at Snow Hill AME Zion Church, is typical of this group of five markers, except for one additional decorative element, an embedded piece of cast-iron, perhaps recycled hardware (Fig. 9). The marker is inscribed:

MEMBR EY
K   P
JANNIE. J.
WIFE OF
W.J. McALIST
ER BORN FEB
29 1902
DIED MAR 2
A.D. 1943

Fig. 9 Concrete marker cast, lettered and decorated by an unidentified maker. Jannie J. McAlister, 1943, Show Hill AME Zion Churchyard, Cumberland County.

The word "MEMBR EY" may be a phonetic misspelling of "member" or "memory" or "remember" or possibly a combination of these words.

Flemington Community Cemetery in rural New Hanover County contains a group of five concrete headstones by this same anonymous craftsman, and a number of unique homemade headstones by other craftsmen, as well as some unusual headstones made of marble. The markers in this cemetery are aligned neatly in rows rather than scattered loosely in the black tradition, probably because the cemetery was moved to its present location. A sizeable black community has used this cemetery since the late nineteenth century. One of the professionally cut marble headstones has this unusual inscription:

EMALINE
WIGGINS
African Slave
Freewoman,
Christian
Died
May 21, 1927

Another professionally cut marble headstone, for Mary E. Johnson (d. 1926), has an epitaph similar to the lyrics of black gospel hymns:

We loved her, Yes we loved her,
But Jesus loved her more, and
He has sweetly called her, to yonder
Shining shore, The Golden Gate
Was open, A gentle Voice said, come
With a fairwell unspoken she calmly
entered home

The most distinctive group of homemade concrete markers in this cemetery is comprised of five creative but crude headstones, painted white, with inscriptions cast with homemade letters, and death dates from 1937 to 1951. The marker for Lazurs Underwood (d. 1943) has a single large flower cast in relief at its top; the little marker for Georgie Spicer (d.

M. Ruth Little

1946) has an awkwardly scalloped top; and the headstone for Richard T. Nixon (d. 1951) has an even more unresolved shape--an undulating top which gives the impression that the concrete is still flowing. The boldest design, used on the headstone for Mrs. Irene Dry (d. 1937) and Mrs. Flora Spears (d. 1950), has three cast semicircular floral rondels at the top (Fig. 10).

Isolated examples of concrete headstones hand-crafted in a folk tradition occur in black graveyards throughout North Carolina. These are almost always painted white. Two of the concrete markers in Cumberland County are inscribed with metal lettering purchased from a hardware store: the headstone for Carolin Williams (d. 1964 at age 101) in the Oak

Fig. 10 One of a group of distinctive markers by an unidentified gravestone maker. Mrs. Flora Spears, 1950, Flemington Community Cemetery, New Hanover County.

Fig. 11 Keyhole concrete marker with lettering on metal tracks. O.A. Melvin, 1961, China Grove Baptist Churchyard, Cumberland County.

M. Ruth Little

Grove Community Graveyard has metal letters and numerals glued to its surface; and the marker for O.A. Melvin (d. 1961), in China Grove Baptist Church, is a tall keyhole-shaped headstone on a high concrete base, with letters and numerals arranged in two metal tracks like the name and address on a rural mailbox (Fig. 11).

Orange County, in the piedmont, has several interesting homemade markers noted during random fieldwork. A bird was drawn in the wet concrete of each arm of the cross-shaped headstone for Marvin Sims (d. 1926) at Mt. Gilead Churchyard. Traces of blue paint outline the birds, and a scene of bushes or trees is painted near the base of the cross. The small concrete headstone for Albert Browder (d. 1945) and his wife Lela (d. 1958), in Mt. Bright Baptist Churchyard in Hillsborough, has an actual pocket watch embedded in the concrete. Although the hands are now missing, rust marks show that their position was at 5:30, probably the time of death. Corrugated metal strips are embedded in the concrete to form stars and other decorative patterns in the tympanum. In a rural black community graveyard in Hillsborough, two concrete crosses have inscriptions that are professionally engraved on brass plaques embedded in the concrete. The cross for Gery Morgan (d. 1939) has a large seashell embedded in each arm. The other cross, for Dilroy and Samuel Harrison (d. 1944), is decorated with an embedded seashell and three stars cast in relief and painted yellow--the seashell and a star on the cross's vertical post and a star on each arm.

The two most interesting black folk headstones recorded in the piedmont county of Davidson are made of concrete and decorated with bits of mirror and stained glass. The concrete headstone for Emma Verdell (d. 1937), in Buncombe Baptist Churchyard in Petersville, uses mirror fragments in a manner similar to that used to decorate an evocative headstone described by a Georgia folklorist. On the Georgia stone is the mark of a human hand with a piece of mirror embedded in its palm[10], while the slender Verdell headstone, with its pointed tympanum and molded border, has its surface embedded with crudely cut mirror fragments in the shapes of a quarter-moon and stars (Fig. 12). Emma Verdell moved to a community of ex-slaves in Petersville in the early twentieth century from Alberton, Georgia.[11]

A headstone using stained glass may be found in the Old Smith Grove Baptist Churchyard in Davidson County. Both this headstone and its footstone are hand-crafted of concrete and pierced by panels of translucent blue stained glass set in lead muntins (Fig. 13). Both markers are painted white, and neither is inscribed.

Fig. 12 Concrete marker decorated with moon and stars cut from mirror. Emma Verdell, 1937, Buncombe Baptist Churchyard, Petersville, Davidson County.

Fig. 13 Uninscribed concrete headstone and footmarker painted white and inlaid with panels of blue glass. Old Smith Grove Baptist Churchyard, Davidson County.

Not only metal and glass but even marble, the pre-eminent material of professional gravestones, is recycled in black graveyards. In a small number of black graveyards in New Hanover and Cumberland and Davidson Counties, fragments of marble, perhaps reused from other gravstones or from demolished buildings, serve as gravemarkers. At Buncombe Baptist Churchyard in Petersville, Davidson County, a broken slab of countertop marble, with no inscription, serves as a headstone. Most reused marble markers are not inscribed, but in Flemington Cemetery an interesting example, which has one molded edge and was apparently part of a marble ledger, is inscribed in an artistic but amateurish lettering style:

    Earhbow Hainelt
    BORNE 1814
    DIED AUG. 1ST, 1888
        The
     Mother of [   ]
    Armstrong and John James.

Grave Enclosures

The third most common type of black gravemarker, the grave enclosure, occurs exclusively in eastern North Carolina. In white graveyards nineteenth-century graves are occasionally surrounded with a cast-iron, marble or wooden railing, or "paling," but the usual custom was to enclose the entire family plot rather than the individual grave. In black graveyards the unit enclosed is usually the individual grave. The boundary takes the form of a low cinderblock wall, a low metal or plastic fence or a border of bricks, shells, rocks or even wooden stakes (Fig. 14).

Decorative concrete blocks often enclose the graves in New Hanover County. The grave of James F. Little (d. 1964), in the Hill Graveyard in Wilmington, is enclosed by a solid concrete block border ten inches high. On the west end of the border, three large pierced concrete blocks form a headpiece, and two identical blocks on the east end form the footpiece (Fig. 15). These pierced blocks are commercial imitations of the concrete screen used in the Indian-inspired architecture of Edward Durrell Stone in the 1950s and 1960s. A metal identification plaque supplied by the funeral home and centered in front of the headpiece is the only inscription. A number of similar grave borders, also painted white, occur in Hank's Chapel AME Churchyard and the Freeman Community Graveyard. The double grave of Mamie and James Franks (d. 1958 and 1956), in Zion Chapel Cemetery, is lined with commercial concrete coping blocks, and the inscription on the homemade concrete headstone is lettered with white chalk or tile grout. In both New Hanover and Cumberland Counties flower garden fencing of metal and plastic encloses individual graves. The same type of fence encloses entire family plots in some rural white graveyards.

Fig. 14   Grave enclosures made of cement blocks and flower garden fencing. Hank's Chapel AME Churchyard, New Hanover County.

Fig. 15   Cement block grave enclosure with headstone and footpiece made of large pierced blocks. An identification plaque is centered between the three head blocks. James F. Little, 1964, Hill Graveyard, Wilmington, New Hanover County.

Grave Sculpture

The fourth and least common type of gravemarker for blacks is three-dimensional "found sculpture." Three unique gravemarkers in eastern North Carolina fit into this category of non-traditional funerary sculpture. Each seems to relate personally to the deceased and to be the product of a spontaneous moment of inspiration. The fact that the markers exist testifies to a tradition of freedom in grave decoration among blacks that is not evident in markers for whites.

The first of these sculptures is a wooden ladder that extends from a grave, apparently representing a ladder to Heaven. This is said to be located in a black churchyard in Menola community in west Hertford County, in the Albemarle region.[12] The second grave sculpture is in the cemetery of Swans Creek Baptist Church in Cumberland County. The grave of William Rudolph Coachman (d.1966) is marked by a government-issue marble headstone which notes his service in World War II as "TEC 5 4380 TRK CO." Marking the foot of Coachman's grave is an automobile wheel rim topped with a decorative arrangement of socket wrenches and plastic flowers (Fig. 16). He was apparently an automobile mechanic, and the sculpture is a strongly personalized statement of his vocation or avocation. Occupational symbols are traditional grave decoration in West Africa and other areas.[13]

Finally, in a black community cemetery in north New Hanover County, a styrofoam chair decorated with greenery and flowers sits at the head of an otherwise unidentified grave (Fig. 17). Although its professional construction suggests that the chair may have been made by a funeral home, perhaps as a custom order, it is an unorthodox grave decoration. Its presence gives the grave a domestic security, as if the chair is keeping watch over the grave or is a symbolic resting place for the deceased.

Fig. 16 Government issue marble headstone, with a footmarker made of an automobile wheel rim, wrenches and plastic flowers. William Randolph Coachman, 1966, Swans Creek Baptist Churchyard, Cumberland County.

Fig. 17 Styrofoam chair with greenery and flowers marking the head of an unidentified grave. Northern New Hanover County, near Pender County line, west side of US 17.

M. Ruth Little

Conclusion

This sampling of Afro-American gravemarkers in North Carolina represents a start toward understanding the Afro-American contribution to the material culture of gravemarkers. These folk grave mounds, headstones, grave enclosures and grave sculptures stand out starkly from typical mass-produced marble and granite stones in twentieth century graveyards, both white and black, which are so uniform in design that neither religious denomination, class status nor geographic location is discernible. It is often impossible to distinguish a black grave mound or headstone from a white one, but a white grave enclosure or grave sculpture is readily distinguishable from a black one. White enclosures are of expensive materials such as cast-iron and brick; white grave sculptures are of marble and granite. Black grave enclosures are made of inexpensive, often recycled materials such as concrete blocks or wood, and black grave sculpture often exhibits creative symbolism, such as the use of a wheel rim and socket wrench as a mechanic's footmarker. A consistent distinction between white and black graveyards is the overall grave layout. White graves are parallel to one another and aligned in even rows; black graves are loosely scattered. The primary distinction between markers for whites and blacks is that those for whites are bound more tightly by popular aesthetic norms than those for blacks.

This creative, fragile artistic tradition deserves documentation. Perhaps this exploration in North Carolina will stimulate fieldwork in other areas of the United States with an Afro-American cultural legacy, and a comparison of the findings made here with black graveyards in other parts of the south to see whether there is a general theme running through the twentieth-century black experience and heritage.

NOTES

1. Works dealing specifically with Afro-American graveyards are sparse. The most useful references for Afro-American gravemarkers are: John M. Vlach, *The Afro-American Tradition in Decorative Arts* (Cleveland: Cleveland Museum of Art, 1978); John D. Combes, "Ethnography, Archaeology and Burial Practices among Coastal South Carolina Blacks," *Conference on Historic Site Archaeology Papers* 7 (1972), 52-61; Robert Farris Thompson, "African Influence on the Art of the United States," *Black Studies in the University*, eds. Armstead L.Robinson et al. (New Haven and London: Yale University Press, 1969); Thompson and Joseph Cornet, *The Four Moments of the Sun: Kongo Art in Two Worlds*, catalogue of exhibit, August 30, 1981-January 17, 1982 (Washington, D.C.: National Gallery of Art, 1982); and Elizabeth A. Fenn, "Honoring the Ancestors: Kongo-American Graves in the American South," *Southern Exposure* 1985 13(5):42-47. William Edmondson, a native of Nashville, Tennessee, was born about 1883 of parents who had been slaves. Serving as a railroad worker, fireman and hospital orderly, he took up the carving of gravemarkers of limestone in the 1930s. He became a prominent sculptor, and his work was displayed at the Museum of Modern Art in New York and the Jeu de Paume in Paris. *William Edmondson: A Restrospective*, the catalogue of an exhibition of his work organized by the Tennessee Arts Commission (Nashville, Tenn., 1981) contains a description of his gravestone work, with a full bibliography, by John Michael Vlach (19-29).

2. In his very useful study "Rural Southern Gravestones: Sacred Artifacts in the Upland South," which appeared in *Markers IV*, ed. David Watters (1987), Gregory Jeane does not distinguish between white and black graveyards and markers. This is undoubtedly because traditional black culture is concentrated in the Lowland South, the coastal areas where the blacks were brought as slaves to work the plantations of the region. The two counties in this North Carolina study where most of the black graveyards were recorded, New Hanover and Cumberland, are Lowland counties. The Upland, piedmont counties of North Carolina have smaller black populations, and only systematic fieldwork, not random sampling, would record rural black graveyards there.

3. John M. Vlach, *The Afro-American Tradition in Decorative Arts*; Robert Farris Thompson and Joseph Cornet, *The Four Moments of the Sun: Kongo Art in Two Worlds*; Thompson, "African Influence on the Art of the United States"; and Elizabeth A. Fenn, "Honoring the Ancestors: Kongo-American Graves in the American South" (note 1).

4. Personal interview with members of the Burns family, Cumberland County, 23 October 1981.

5. Vlach 1978 (note 1).

M. Ruth Little

6. Personal interview with Mr. Shaw, Shaw Funeral Home, Wilmington, N.C., December 1982.

7. Personal interviews with Hazel Culbreth, widow of Renial Culbreth, and their children, Mary Julia and Renial George, 5 August 1981 and 9 July 1982.

8. The only patternbook which I found during the inventory was a small pamphlet used by Doug Buchanan, who operates a one-man monument company in Newland, N.C., in the Blue Ridge Mountains. The brochure contains photographs of twelve different gravestone designs, presumably supplied by one of the monument companies in Elberton, Georgia, where Buchanan buys his granite.

9. Personal interview with Issiah McEachin, Eastover, N.C., 9 July 1982.

10. Thompson 1969 (note 1) 152.

11. Telephone interview with Mrs. Beatrice Clodfelter, Petersville, N.C., 23 June 1982.

12. Personal interview with Roy Johnson, Johnson Publishing Company, Murfreesboro, N.C., 7 February 1981.

13. Thompson and Cornet 1982 (note 1).

Fig. 1 Potter Palmer family mausoleum, Graceland Cemetery.

COMMUNITIES OF THE DEAD:
TOMBSTONES AS A REFLECTION OF SOCIAL ORGANIZATION

Paula J. Fenza

The primary purpose of archaeology is to reconstruct extinct social systems on the basis of the physical remains left behind by a vanished society. One of the most fruitful archaeological sources of information about social organization is mortuary data. According to Lewis Binford (1971, 208), "Human burials are one of the most frequently encountered classes of cultural feature observed by archeologists." Because burial practices stress attitudes toward life and death, the study of them reveals valuable insights on how the society that practiced them organized itself. Joseph Tainter (1978, 329) states: "Indeed, to the extent to which a mortuary population contains individuals who held membership in the various structural components of a system, one can expect the mortuary population to reflect the structure of the extinct society."

To this end, many archaeologists have developed analytical models for inferring social organization from mortuary data. A common theme of these models is the equation of social status with the material expenditure found in the burial. According to all these models, it is possible to define the levels of social status in a society according to the different mortuary treatments accorded different individuals.

Each theory presupposes that increased expenditure of material resources in a burial indicates increased social status of the individual interred. By the same token, the levels of expenditure in the general treatment of a cemetery, or a portion thereof, are likely to reflect the status of the society represented in that cemetery or in that portion. These conclusions may be modified by another factor, that of symbolism appearing on, or in the form of, the gravemarker, reflecting the status of the deceased or the group in society to which he/she belonged when living. The purpose of this paper is to test these theories using data collected in contemporary cemeteries in the Chicago area.

To insure that the study sample reflects a midwestern, urban orientation, all the cemeteries included in this study are located within the city limits of Chicago or in the collar suburbs immediately surrounding the city (Table 1). These peripheral cemeteries were established in the late nineteenth century and attest to the influence of the rural cemetery movement (Warner 1959) as, at the time of their founding, they were located in the rural area surrounding the actual city. Sizes of the cemeteries range from very small (St. James of the Sag, less than 100 burials) to very large (Forest Home, 180,000 burials). Most are of moderate size, ranging from 30,000 to 80,000 burials.

The tombstones used in this study cover a hundred-year time span, from approximately 1880 to 1987 (Table 1). Chicago did not begin to develop as a major urban center until the post-Civil War industrial boom; indeed, the real growth of Chicago as a city can be dated to its rebuilding after the great Chicago Fire of 1871. Consequently, its major cemeteries were also established during this period of urban growth and reflect the emergence of a new social structure, one based on the rapid influx of immigrants attracted to a ready source of jobs and the birth of a new monied elite seeking ways to validate their status (Sawyers 1986, 7). Therefore, although the cemeteries in this study comprise a wide spectrum of ethnic, religious, and socio-economic levels, they are representative of a midwestern, urban, industrial population.

The advantages of using these data are twofold. First, since the material culture is augmented by written records, it is possible to verify assumptions made on the basis of the material culture against the ethnographic data. Second, since in American society pertinent data on burial custom in the form of tombstones is readily accessible, information can be collected by simple survey methods.

For purposes of this study size and cost of the monuments were criteria used in assessing material expenditure. It is a defensible argument that in American society cost is often a valid measure of the status value of an item. Therefore, cost of a monument is very likely a reliable measure of its (and its owner's) prestige. Application of this guideline to the data produced the five types of material expenditure described below. A sixth factor, that of symbolism, is then discussed.

1. **Dynastic mausoleums.** Dynastic mausoleums are so titled because of their extended family orientation; in additon to the founding "head" of the family and his spouse, the mausoleum contains their children, the childrens' spouses, sometimes grandchildren, and occasionally the grandchildren's spouses. There is a conscious attempt to recreate in the cemetery the kind of dynastic affiliations that existed in life.

Material expenditure in the production of dynastic mausoleums is apparent. Even a cursory examination of the mausoleums in Graceland Cemetery on Chicago's near north side reveals strong evidence of wealth. Mausoleums are large and made of expensive materials. They are embellished with fine original sculptures and reproductions of classical statuary. Stylistically they show great variation based on the artistic or architectural styles popular in the living community. For example, the mausoleum of the Potter Palmer family built during the Greek Revival period of the 1890s is a facsimile of a Greek temple, not much smaller than the original after which it was modeled (Fig. 1). It is faced with marble and supported by Corinthian columns. The Honore family, across the path from the Palmers, is interred in a miniature medieval cathedral. The Getty mausoleum, designed by Louis Sullivan, is as elegant as any of the buildings he designed. Oak Woods Cemetery, on the edge of Hyde Park on Chicago's south side, also contains a number of fine dynastic mausoleums, including many of the founders of the University of Chicago

In addition to their construction, dynastic mausoleums also reflect material expenditure in their surroundings. The plots on which they are situated are large and well landscaped. Carefully tended shrubbery accents the structures. The mausoleums frequently overlook desirable natural features such as the lagoons at Graceland or Bronswood in west suburban Oak Brook.

2. **Dynastic burial**. Like dynastic mausoleums, dynastic burials also have an extended family orientation. The layout consists of a family marker in the center of the plot surrounded by smaller markers of individual family members. The central markers are large and made of expensive materials. As with dynastic mausoleums, the range of stylistic variation is great. A monumental sculpture by Loredo Taft entitled "Eternal Silence" presides over the Graves family plot in Graceland (Fig. 2). Another plot features a seven-foot natural granite boulder with the family name engraved on it. Again, plots are large and luxuriously landscaped. Plots are frequently surrounded by low stone curbing or wrought iron fencing to separate them from their neighbors. As with dynastic mausoleums, dynastic burials may also take advantage of pleasing natural features. The graves of Daniel Burnham and his family (Fig. 3) are located on a small island in the center of the lagoon at Graceland, a fitting tribute to the man who did so much to develop Chicago's lakefront.

Both dynastic mausoleums and dynastic burials, then, are characterized by stylistic variation based on personal choice and cultural aesthetics, spaciousness, advantageous positioning, and choice construction materials. It is not surprising, in reading the names on the dynastic monuments described here, to verify that they represent the leading lights of Chicago's

Fig. 2   Graves family plot, Graceland Cemetery. "Eternal Silence" sculpture by Loredo Taft.

Fig. 3 Daniel Burnham family graves, Graceland Cemetery.

gilded age--the founders, the developers, the industrial giants, and the social and political leaders of the city. In their lives these people gloried in luxury and conspicuous ostentation; in death they occupy the same position.

3. **Non-dynastic mausoleums**. Non-dynastic mausoleums are so named because there is no extended family orientation. Small mausoleums usually consist of only two burials, usually husband and wife. Non-dynastic mausoleums are much smaller and less varied than their dynastic counterparts. Although attractive, they are much more stylistically homogenous; usually only a few conventional styles are repeated. The plots on which they are located are much smaller and do not make use of formal landscaping. Materials used in construction are also more common; they

do not take advantage of rare resources. Forest Home Cemetery in west suburban Forest Park contains many examples of non-dynastic mausoleums (Fig. 4).

4. Non-dynastic burials. Like non-dynastic mausoleums, non-dynastic burials do not have an extended family orientation. Plots contain the burials of husband and wife. Occasionally sub-adult or unmarried children are buried with their parents, but the inclusion of married children and their spouses is rare.

Fig. 4 A "non-dynastic mausoleum" for the Chilcher family, Forest Home Cemetery.

Paula J. Fenza

There are no central family markers in non-dynastic burials, only individual stones. Monuments are smaller and generally all the same size. A few are slightly larger than the rest and may belong to more prominent members of the community; however, these do not begin to approach the size of even the more modest stones of dynastic burials. Stylistically they are also not as diverse; they repeat a few common, mass-produced styles. Nor are they decorated with original artwork; engravings are simple and conventional.

Layout of non-dynastic burials is also simple. Graves are not landscaped and do not take advantage of pleasing natural features. They are arranged in straight rows rather than pursuing individual choice or orientation. Plots are smaller and closer together; they are not separated by curbing or fencing.

Resurrection Cemetery in south suburban Justice consists of typical non-dynastic burials. It serves an area of Chicago that is highly industrial and has always been demographically middle-income. Its members are drawn from a blue-collar, middle-class population, and its burials reflect this (Fig. 5). In Graceland or Oak Woods one gets a sense of spaciousness and refinement reminiscent of the upper-class Chicago neighborhoods from which their members originally came. Resurrection Cemetery, with its neat, straight rows of homogeneous stones, is equally reminiscent of a neighborhood of middle-class bungalows from the south side of Chicago.

5. **Low-status burials.** Low-status burials represent the minimum in mortuary treatment. Two cemeteries in this sample have examples of low-status burials.

A section of west suburban Elmwood Cemetery in River Grove is reserved for pauper burials. In this section there is no stylistic variation (Fig. 6). All the stones are small and flush with the ground. The lettering is in plain block style. The only information given is the name of the

Fig. 5   Resurrection Cemetery in south suburban Justice.

Fig. 6   Jane McGoogan, 1930, Resurrection Cemetery. A "non-dynastic" burial.

Paula J. Fenza

deceased and the years of birth and death. In some cases even the year of birth is omitted, perhaps unknown. The stones are in short, straight rows with a minimum of space between them. They are also located in a remote, undesirable part of the cemetery next to a utility shed.

Woodlawn Cemetery in west suburban North Riverside is the site of another set of low-status burials. In 1918 a circus train derailed near Chicago, killing many of the circus workers. Their remains were interred in Woodlawn (Fig. 7). Later, the Showmen's League of America purchased this section of the cemetery for burial of other circus personnel (Sarkauskas 1986, 12). These tombstones are also extremely plain and uniform. Information on them is sparse--just the name and years of birth and death. Often the first name is simply a nickname, as if the person's given name were unknown. Again, the year of birth is frequently missing.

Fig. 7 Harold "Buddy" Paddock, 1968, Woodlawn Cemetery. A circus worker's grave.

Rows are straight, and there is minimal space between stones. The only note of decoration is four large stone elephants marking the four corners of the section. The popular conception of "carnies" as nomadic people with no family or social ties is borne out in their cemetery. There is nothing here to connect them with any affiliation other than that of the circus.

There is no variation or complexity among low-status burials. They represent the barest minimum expenditure necessary to inter individuals according to the legal and social mores of society. Plots are small and crowded together; markers give minimal information about the deceased. There is no family orientation, not even that of husband and wife. Low-status burials are the simplest possible form of burial.

The implications of this data, according to archaeological models, are clear. Burials can be divided into three classes. Dynastic mausoleums and dynastic burials form an upper class. It has been demonstrated that they represent maximum material expenditure in midwestern mortuary custom. Size and style of stones, size of plots, and location are all lavish. Ethnographic data supports this conclusion. The individuals interred in the dynastic burials discussed here represent the elite of Chicago society.

Non-dynastic mausoleums and non-dynastic burials are the largest part of this sample and represent the middle class. Energy expenditure is less than that of upper-class burials, but is still at a moderately high level. Size and stylistic variation among middle-class burials is not as elaborate but still allows for a modicum of personal choice. Like the middle class itself, middle-class burials represent a high degree of homogeneity, yet a "comfortable" degree of individuality.

The lower class, represented in low-status burials, is the most insignificant and easily overlooked segment of society. Material expenditure on lower-class burials is minimal. The lower class merits little attention in life and is given equally little attention in mortuary practice.

Paula J. Fenza

Midwestern mortuary practice, then, substantiates a model of material expenditure in mortuary custom as a measure of the rank of the deceased. Three levels of material expenditure are demonstrated in Chicago cemeteries which represent three levels of social status. The number of burials in each level corresponds to demographic data on the living community. Ethnographic and historical records of Chicago verify that the status reflected by their burials correspond to the actual status occupied by these persons in life. A material culture model of social ranking is validated.

6. **Symbolism.** A few minor anomalies in the data, however, point out the need for at least one additional criterion for determining status from mortuary data. Study of the data indicates that an additional criterion, that of symbolism, helps augment and refine the conclusions suggested by the material expenditure model. The following examples illustrate the influence of symbolism as it relates to material expenditure.

In Elmwood Cemetery there is a group of tombstones of Roman Catholic nuns. Although these women undoubtedly came from middle- or even possibly upper-class families, they have low-class tombstones. The stones are small and simple blocks set in straight lines with minimal space between them. The only information recorded is the nun's religious name and the dates of her birth and death (Fig. 8). They represent minimum material expenditure and, according to a material culture model, have low social rank. Yet nuns are a highly respected segment of society and considered to have a higher status than their tombstones suggest. However, these women espoused a vocation that preached the virtues of poverty, humility, and conformity. The symbolic poverty of their tombstones, then, is a reflection of religious doctrine.

Communities of the Dead

A second example of symbolism concerns gypsy burials. The gypsy burials in Forest Home Cemetery in Forest Park make a fascinating ethnic study. Gypsy graves present unusual characteristics. Even though gypsies are not a high-class group, their tombstones are very large and ornate and are engraved with numerous religious symbols including saints, madonnas, Jesus Christ, the Cross, and other examples of Christian iconography (Fig. 9). The plots themselves are also large. But the most unusual feature of gypsy graves is the use of grave goods (Fig. 10). All major holidays are represented by grave decorations--flags on Independence Day, miniature Christmas trees at Christmas, colored eggs, Easter baskets, jelly beans, and chocolate rabbits at Easter. Offerings of food and drink at other times of the year are also common. Bags of snack foods, slices of birthday cake, bottles of whiskey or wine (complete with paper cups), cans of beer, cups of coffee, packs of cigarettes, and candy are just some of the items which the author has found.

Fig. 8   Graves of three Roman Catholic nuns, Elmwood Cemetery.

Fig. 9   Gypsy graves, Forest Home Cemetery.

Fig. 10   Grave goods on a gypsy tomb, Forest Home Cemetery.

These practices become understandable when seen in terms of gypsy attitudes toward death. Gypsies fear death and the dead. They believe that death is an unnatural occurrence and that the dead are resentful at having died. It is thought that the dead will seek revenge on the living for their deaths unless they are made to feel comfortable in death. For this reason gypsies have developed a cemetery cult to placate the spirits of the dead. Funeral celebrations are sumptuous affairs to please the dead; some families have even exhausted personal resources to provide a sufficiently lavish funeral. Favorite personal effects of the deceased are enclosed in the coffin. Families sponsor large memorial feasts, particularly in the first year following death, and sporadically thereafter. Food from the feasts is taken to the grave site so the deceased can join in the celebration. Offerings are also left at other times to keep the dead satisfied in their graves. For the same reason the dead are included in holiday celebrations. Families visit the grave regularly, either to bring food or to communicate with the dead through quiet meditation (Trigg 1973).

Fig. 11 William L. Patterson, 1980, Forest Home Cemetery. A socialist's grave.

Paula J. Fenza

Seen within the context of gypsy ethnic beliefs, the apparent anomaly of high-class stones used by a low-class group becomes clearer. Large plots, ornate stones, elaborate engravings, and grave goods are a means by which gypsy ghosts are placated and kept happy in their graves.

A third type of symbolism may also be found in Forest Home Cemetery. In 1886 none of Chicago's other cemeteries would receive the bodies of the four victims hanged for allegedly conspiring to incite the Haymarket Riot. Forest Home was the only place willing to offer burial space. After Emma Goldman, the noted socialist, chose to be buried with the Haymarket victims, surrounding plots became the traditional resting place for other Chicago socialists, such as William L. Patterson (Fig. 11). The tombstones in this section reflect their owners' socialist philosophy just as strongly as the stones in Graceland reflect a capitalist philosophy. All the stones are the same size and set flush to the ground. Space between them is minimal. In addition to pertinent information about the deceased, each stone bears a socialist motto. Some of the more common are: "working class hero," "communist leader," "a life dedicated to human freedom," and "tireless fighter for socialism." The socialist creed of a classless society is well demonstrated in their burials. Although the individuals themselves were generally of the middle class, they chose low-class stones as a political statement.

A final point on symbolism concerns the position of women in midwestern society, as indeed elsewhere. Superficially there does not appear to be any difference between men and women within classes. Each is accorded the same level of material expenditure, and from this it can be inferred that men and women are of equal status within classes. However, there are subtle differences in the symbolism on women's stones which suggest that women may, in fact, occupy a secondary status in relation to that of men. Women are rarely given professional attribution, although the mention of professional status on men's stones is common. A pair of stones in Graceland illustrates this quite well. Timothy Webster and Kate Warn were two Pinkerton detectives who foiled an assassination plot against Abraham Lincoln in 1861. Their stones are located with Allan Pinkerton's in his family plot. Webster's stone describes his professional activity in great detail (Fig. 12); Warn's stone, immediately adjacent to Webster's, lists only her name and dates of birth and death. Her professional status would be unknown if not mentioned on the stones of Webster and Pinkerton.

Fig. 12 Timothy Webster, Graceland Cemetery. A Pinkerton detective who foiled a plot against Abraham Lincoln.

Paula J. Fenza

Women are also described in more emotional terms than men i.e., "my beloved," "my darling wife," and women are more frequently referred to only in terms of their relationship to some other person i.e., "wife of," and "mother of" are common; "husband of," and "father of" are not (Fig. 13).

The foregoing examples demonstrate that although material expenditure does reflect aspects of social organization, symbolism on the stones may also be an important criterion in determining status. In all of these examples symbolism on the stones is as important as the money spent in producing them. It has been recognized by several researchers (Huntington and Metcalf 1979; Hertz 1973; Aries 1974, 1975) that symbolism is an integral part of mortuary custom. A valid model, therefore, must consider both symbolism and material expenditure as indications of social status.

Fig. 13 Agnes Kruesinca and Annie Ritzma, 1957, 1963, described in terms of marital relationship.

This paper represents an initial approach to defining an anthropological model of midwestern mortuary custom. The ultimate goal of this research is to develop a model which integrates the study of both material expenditure and types of symbols used as a means of defining social status. Statistical analysis of the data may reveal co-varying attributes whose presence or absence reinforces the significance of each other. For example, the kinds of symbols used on typical upper-class stones (such as those in Graceland) are usually secular, classical, and a reflection of prevailing aesthetic standards. This emphasizes that the aberrant religious symbolism of gypsy stones is indicative of a nonconforming subgroup. Even without knowing the ethnology of gypsy attitudes toward death, the overt religious symbolism and use of grave goods, not present in other burials, are an indication that these burials are a significant variation from the general mortuary pattern. My current research has focused on an urban population. However, cursory examination of some rural cemeteries, approximately 100 miles from the Chicago area, indicates that some of the observations made about urban practices may also hold true for rural practices. Future research will be directed toward developing and refining the model and testing its validity for both urban and rural communities.

TABLE 1

CEMETERIES SURVEYED FOR THIS STUDY

Cemetery	Location
Graceland	Chicago, near north
Oak Woods	Chicago, near south
Bohemian National	Chicago, far north
Resurrection	Chicago, far south
St. James of the Sag	Chicago, far southwest
Forest Home	Forest Park
Woodlawn	North Riverside
Waldheim	North Riverside
Elmwood	River Grove
St. Michael	River Grove
Bronswood	Oak Brook
Mt. Carmel	Hillside
Mt. Auburn Memorial	Stickney

REFERENCES

Phillipe Aries, *Western Attitudes Toward Death from the Middle Ages to the Present* (Baltimore: Johns Hopkins Press, 1974); "The Reversal of Death: Changes in Attitudes Toward Death in Western Societies," *Death in America*, ed. D. Stannard (Philadelphia: University of Pennsylvania Press, 1975).

Lewis Binford, "Mortuary Practices: Their Study and Their Potential," *An Archeological Perspective* (Seminar Press, 1971).

Max Gluckman ed., *Essays on the Ritual of Social Relations* (Manchester: Manchester University Press, 1979).

Jack Goody, *Death, Property, and the Ancestors* (Palo Alto: Stanford University Press, 1962).

Ralph Huntington and Peter Metcalf, *Celebrations of Death: The Anthropology of Mortuary Ritual* (Cambridge: Cambridge University Press, 1979).

Susan Sarkauskas, "Some History Close to Home," *Cicero Life*, September 14, 1986.

June Sawyers, "A Resting Place for History," *Chicago Tribune*, September 5, 1986.

Arthur Saxe, *Social Dimensions of Mortuary Practice* (Unpublished Ph.D. dissertation, University of Michigan, 1970).

Joseph Tainter, "Modeling Change in Prehistoric Social Systems," *For Theory Building in Archeology*, ed. L. Binford (New York: Academic Press, 1977). "Mortuary Practices and the Study of Prehistoric Social Systems," *Advances in Archeological Method and Theory* (New York: Academic Press, 1978), 1:105-141.

Edward Trigg, *Gypsy Demons and Divinities* (Secausus, NJ: Citadel Press, 1973).

Victor Turner, *The Forest of Symbols* (Ithaca, NY: Cornell University Press, 1967). *The Ritual Process* (Ithaca, NY: Cornell University Press, 1977).

William Warner, *The Living and the Dead* (New Haven: Yale University Press, 1959).

Fig. 1 Painted concrete statue of Jesus, Espanola.

CAMPOSANTOS: SACRED PLACES OF THE SOUTHWEST

Laura Sue Sanborn*

Not far from our house in New Mexico is the village burial ground of Hispanic Catholics called a camposanto, or "field of the saints." One afternoon I saw a small woman enter the camposanto carrying a basket filled with tinfoil. Later I discovered her work: three wooden crosses neatly sheathed in tin foil and wrapped with rosary beads and ribbons and stuck into a gravemound. There were no names, no dates, no written testaments on these gravemarkers. They were a humble gift of love in a field of such gifts.

The camposanto is different from the cemeteries that most of us know. In the camposanto people may freely express their emotions by creating personal, handmade gravemarkers. These markers constitute a unique collection of religious folk art that reflects both culture and history (Fig. 1). The camposanto is tranquil in its harmony with nature and yet a vibrant and colorful portrait of its people -- both those living and those dead. It is full of human drama, filled with poignant expressions of emotion. The camposanto is a place of change where wind whips sand against

---

* The following article was written in June 1986, after a year of exploring and photographing New Mexican camposantos. The paper remained unpublished. Several months ago I returned to a large camposanto cited in my study only to find that another ten acres of it had been destroyed and turned into a memorial park. My concern for the obliteration of such a precious resource spurred the resurrection of my paper. This paper elaborates upon the special qualities of the camposanto gravemarker, the historical context of which was so aptly provided in Nancy Hunter Warren's article, "New Mexico Village Camposantos" published in *Markers IV*.

sandstone, softening sculpted lines; where jack rabbits and quail are born and die; where paint blisters and peels, only to be repainted by those who play for time against the forces of nature; and where seasons and holidays are celebrated.

As you approach a camposanto, you will notice that the vegetation in the camposanto is indigenous, there is no manicured turf, no irrigation. The desert camposanto may be covered with fragrant sage and dotted with dark green junipers; some are filled with cacti whose bright pink spring flowers further enliven the site. In the mountain camposanto long grasses grow with pinon pine, and boulders jut up among the stone gravemarkers. Visitors to a rural camposanto often find themselves completely cradled by nature; alone with no reminders of civilization other than the messages of the markers. Even those camposantos now surrounded by urban development retain their native vegetation, which harmonizes with the larger landscape of mountains and mesas.

One enters the camposanto through a gate or portal, since all camposantos are enclosed in some way. Some camposantos have both entry and exit gates for funerals, symbolizing the passage of life from one point to another. Printed over one such portal are the words, "Dios da y Dios quita" -- "the Lord gives and the Lord taketh away." In the center of the camposanto a massive cross, often of hewn timbers, symbolizes the sanctity of the place and is the focal point of the enclosure.

Amid the native landscape inside the enclosure one finds the graves. Frequently not only the gravemarker but the entire gravesite is a work of art. Graves may be surrounded by handmade cerquitas (fences) commonly crafted out of wood, wrought iron, or metal pipe (Figs. 2, 3 and 4). One handmade cerquita I found had wrought iron horses prancing at its four corners; another displayed the names of the deceased's children intricately carved on wooden side panels. Old, very ornate, cast-iron cerquitas were ordered by the wealthy from St. Louis and brought in on the railroad.

Fig. 2 Wood cerquita, Albuquerque.

Fig. 3 Metal pipe cerquita, Peralta

Fig. 4   Wood cerquita, Peralta

The variety and ingenuity of the gravemarkers seem endless. You feel compelled to walk past each work of folk art lest you miss some new form of a craftmen's creativity. The first-time visitor to a camposanto will be amazed by the range of materials used to create the gravemarkers and by the exuberance of color and texture. The primary materials are wood, metal, stone, and concrete, although re-used objects are also commonly incorporated. I have found gravemarkers made of, or decorated with: concrete blocks, patio stones, logs, wood rounds, bricks, large tiles, mosaic tiles, wrought iron, water pipe, PVC pipe, horseshoes, a floor grate, a sewer grate, appliance parts, automobile chrome, radiator parts, baby crib parts, ball bearings, glass blocks, marbles, shells, jewelry, a tackle box, earrings, rosaries, buttons, ashtrays, candlesticks, beer and pop cans, bottles, metal drums, jars, vases, pottery, pictures, picture frames, crucifixes, plastic flowers, silk flowers, paper flowers, flower boxes, egg cartons, styrofoam, plastic, rope, chicken wire, barrel rims, saw blades, paint, paint cans, cloth, yarn, ribbon, plastic beads, glass beads, tacks, nails, pins, metallic letters, chunks of turquoise, cogs, gears, pebbles, lava rock, garden fence, broken colored glass, small toys, suncatchers, statuary, porcelain picture discs, pie pans, tin cans, a garden hoe, aluminum foil, astro turf, carpeting, popsicle sticks, sheet metal, shingling, wind chimes, light sockets, buckets, hood ornaments, padlocks, chains, flags, banners, wooden crates, silverware, door knobs, and baby bottles.

The ways in which these materials are used are as fascinating as the range of objects. The floor grate, for instance, was made into a gravemarker by cutting the upturned end into a series of stair-step crosses. Another gravemarker was created by imbedding in a concrete cross a sealed Coke bottle in which a statue of Christ had been placed by sawing off, then re-gluing, the bottom of the bottle. One woman had made a gravemarker for her husband by centering her favorite glass candleholders in the rectangular opening of a formed concrete cross, so that the evening light shone through the glass illuminating the entire marker (Fig. 5). A whimsical child's gravemarker was created out of pink and green patio blocks to look like a giant Easter basket, complete with colored, concrete eggs. Sunshine's grave had been marked by torching her name into a large circular saw blade which was welded to some machinery parts for a base. Ramon's marker was created by pouring concrete into the grill area of an old Model T Ford which served as a frame. Someone long ago had carefully split and splayed the ends of some pinon boards to create a delicate fan-shaped cross.

Fifteen of the most fascinating gravemarkers in one camposanto are the work of a man who fashioned chrome cages for the graves of his friends and family. He decorated these elaborate and sometimes multi-tiered cages with chains, padlocks, bolts, flags, rows of radiator caps, and metal nail-punched signs with messages such as "God is Love," "My God, My

Fig. 5   A recent cross made of glass candleholders, Peralta.

Fig. 6   Early wood gravemarker, Peralta.

God, You Have Forsaken Me," "Lock the Gate," and "Visitors Welcome to Take Pictures." Bolted to each gravemarker are from two to five plaques bearing the maker's name or initials.

Some personalized gravesites may lead us to speculate upon the character of the craftsman or upon the character of the deceased, such as the man whose grave is decorated with statues of horses and cowboys, whiskey bottles and a lariat. Collectively, the creators' choice of materials, colors, forms, symbols, words and spatial arrangement provide clues to a people's history and culture. Such choices are especially significant because the creators have not been biased or inhibited by formal design training.

The earliest camposanto gravemarkers, which were made of wood, date back to the mid-1800s (Fig. 6). Prior to that time the poor were buried in unmarked graves, and the wealthy were buried in the church floor, with the church itself providing a monument of status.

Early wood gravemarkers became more elaborate when traders arrived in New Mexico with improved woodworking tools. Although many of the wooden markers have completely decayed, most camposantos still have an old section of weather-worn wooden crosses. Two of the most remarkable wood markers I found stand like Easter Island sentinels dominating an isolated rocky island. These giant slabs of wood, a precious commodity in the desert, have weathered to a silver grey and show the patterns where plaques are discernible--they stand as a mute testament to the status of those interred in their shadow.

Traders also brought iron into New Mexico, which craftsmen formed into more durable crosses and cerquitas (Fig. 7). Stone gravemarkers did not become popular until the 1880s, when a wave of immigrants arrived in New Mexico with the railroad. Among the immigrants were French and Italian stonecutters, who were brought in to embellish public buildings, but who also carved marble headstones for the wealthy. Local people copied this art in local materials--sandstone and limestone. Stone markers, like those of wood and iron, range from the humble to the ornate, with some no more than a boulder incised with a crude cross or initials (Fig. 8).

Gravemarker materials have continued to reflect the material culture of the time. Concrete has remained the most popular material since the turn of the century because it is easy to form and decorate and relatively durable. Gravemarkers made in the 1950s have been fashioned of large glass ashtrays, chrome car parts, hood ornaments, and white and black enameled appliance parts. An influx of the hippie culture of the 1960s is evident on gravemarkers decorated with peace signs and love beads. Flower decoration has changed from paper to plastic, and silk flowers appear more frequently. The use of some other decorative materials is rooted in ancient tradition. For example, the colored tile mosaics covering some gravemarkers represent Moorish art brought from Spain.

Fig. 7   Iron cross, old section of Peralta camposanto.

Fig. 8　Simple stone marker, Galisteo.

The camposantos are colorful places, not only because of the materials used, but also because many markers are brightly painted. Light blue, pink, green, red-orange and silver are the most popular colors. Murals or religious scenes are sometimes painted on markers, or on a concrete slab covering the entire gravesite. Paint brightens grey machine-made markers, with the etched figures filled in like a coloring book. The use of bright colors, according to Terry Jordan in his book, *Texas Graveyards; A Cultural Legacy*, can be traced to Spain, where camposantos are still brightly colored, or to Mexico where "the use of color in a sacred context has ample pre-Columbian precedent," and "where even huge pyramids once bore bright paints".[1]

Fig. 9 Freshly white-washed markers at an Albuquerque camposanto.

Laura Sue Sanborn

Forms and symbols also provide cultural clues. Jordan notes in his study of Texas cemeteries that any sort of religious symbolism is anathema to the theologies of Calvin, Wesley, and Knox and that therefore the gravemarkers of these religious groups are devoid of crosses or crucifixes. In the camposanto, however, religious symbolism abounds. Almost all gravemarkers are either in the form of the cross or are decorated with crosses and crucifixes. Often three or four crosses are stuck in the gravemound along with rosaries, statues, and framed pictures of Christ, Mary, and patron saints. Other common camposanto symbols included the heart--long a symbol of love (Fig. 9); the Pascal Lamb--often seen on children's stones; the dove--representing the soul's peaceful ascension into heaven; and, in one village camposanto a deathshead design similar to those on early New England headstones.

Less literal symbols, such as the five- and six-pointed stars and daisies prevalent in some Hispanic markers, reflect the influence of other cultures. Jordan believes that the Hispanics adopted the star symbol from German immigrants who thought it to be a "witches foot" hex sign for warding off "evil spirits and the Devil."[2] Some older markers are so covered with these symbols that they emanate an eerie mysticism (Fig. 10).

A fascinating gesture found in some camposantos stems from old Navajo and Pueblo Indian traditions. The gravemounds are either completely covered with the deceased's dishes and pottery, deliberately broken over the grave to symbolically break the chain of death in a family, or intact, placed there by the family so that the deceased may use them in the afterlife. Knick-knacks, clothing, favorite belongings, and even the contents of the deceased's refrigerator, sometimes appear on the gravemound, giving the burial ground an appearance surprising to the uninitiated visitor.

Fig. 10 Old stone marker with hearts, stars, crescent moon and tree-of-life, Tecolote camposanto.

Other gravesite objects suggest varying explanations as to meaning and origin. A door plate and knob found on one grave may be a symbolic door to heaven, or perhaps it is just the doorknob from the deceased's home. A light socket imbedded in a concrete marker may have contained a bulb which symbolically lighted the deceased's way to the after-world, just as some Swiss still hang lanterns on graves for that purpose today, or it may be a sign of status for a family fortunate enough to have electricity.

Decorative symbols are used far more extensively than words, especially on the older markers, which sometimes have no more than a cross, a name, or a date. The abundance of misspelled words and reversed letters, which sometimes make a marker look like a tablet in ancient Greek, indicates difficulty with the written language, especially if written in English. One cannot help but smile at the carefully carved child's stone that reads, "For My Little Angle."

Not only the markers themselves but their arrangement as well can provide insight. The spatial organization of the camposantos stresses the individual rather than the family. Curbed or fenced family plots with large family markers, which are common in Anglo cemeteries, are rarely found in the camposanto. Instead, the individual's grave is curbed or fenced. Man and wife do not necessarily lie side by side, and the children are often relegated to a separate section. A particularly disturbing area of some camposantos is the limbo area, containing an array of small concrete blocks which mark the graves of unbaptized babies whose souls can go to neither heaven nor hell. Grave alignment is important in many religions, with "feet to the east" the most common Christian burial pattern, reflecting a belief in Christ's resurrection in the east.[3] The Hispanic Catholic burial, however, does not favor any particular alignment. I have found burials aligned in all compass directions as well as facing the main road, facing the central cross, facing downslope on a hill, and facing secondary lanes within the camposanto. Several camposantos have gravemarkers which face in four or more distinctly different directions. Susan Hazen-Hammond, who has studied the camposantos for the past seven years, writes that the lack of a distinct orientation may reflect the belief that "since life is not orderly, why should death be?"[4]

Camposantos are places where life is celebrated not forgotten. Anna Marie kneels in the parted sage repainting her grandfather's name under the hot noon sun with the only tool she has -- a toothpick. Mr. Romero brings a favorite baseball and places it on his son's ten-year-old grave. The Martinez family has gathered to braid bright new ribbons through the iron bars of a child's cerquita and to whitewash the boulders outlining family graves. Nearby a new banner on a gravemound is lettered with the words, "I love you Grandpa."

During the Christmas season decorated Christmas trees are set at the foot of some graves. Garlands, wreaths, Christmas ornaments, and toys are placed at the headstones (Figs. 11 and 12). Last Christmas, while wandering through a camposanto aglow with luminaries, I found two small, red, toy-filled stockings propped up against the headstones of a baby brother and sister. At Easter new crucifixes appear, lilies are planted, and ceramic Easter bunnies and eggs are left on graves. Stryofoam hearts covered with red plastic roses are left for deceased wives and sweethearts on Valentine's Day. And attached to the cerquita of Maria Teresa were the shriveled remains of a pink balloon on a string and a "Happy Birthday" party napkin.

Despite their significant human value, something dismaying is happening to some camposantos: they are being destroyed. Camposantos in urban areas are falling victim to land use pressures and the lure of higher economic returns. Camposantos have been paved over for parking lots and built over for condominiums and commercial development. Recently nearly 3,000 bodies were reinterred so that a camposanto could be mined for its sand and gravel deposits. Last year I watched as bulldozers ravaged

Fig. 11   Grave decorated for the holidays, Albuquerque.

Fig. 12   Grave gifts, Peralta.

a camposanto, destroying hundreds of handmade gravemarkers so that the area could be turned into a memorial park cemetery. Rows of wooden, stone, and wrought iron crosses were gouged from places once sanctified by their presence. By the time the workmen were finished, fifteen hundred graves had been scraped bare. The rich and colorful diversity of handmade markers which had been so lovingly crafted are gone forever.

Now the native vegetation which was home to a wealth of urban wildlife has been replaced with sod which must be mowed and irrigated with water--a precious resource. Now, instead of the highly personal handmade markers, only uniform machine-made markers which lie flush with the grass are permitted. The camposanto, a unique part of the southwestern landscape, has been replaced by the generic memorial park.

One day while photographing this camposanto destruction, I asked the cemetery superintendent why it was happening. He answered, "Money," and went on to explain that "once we've got sod and water in here, people have to pay for it--you know--perpetual care. And they have to buy the headstones, too." Then, pointing to a few remaining handmade crosses lying in the sagebrush he added, "You can't make any money on this stuff."

Unfortunately, little or no protection exists for the camposantos. The National Register of Historic Places recognizes only cemeteries of national significance derived from association with historic renown (such as Gettysburg and Arlington National Cemetery), or of exceptional architectural design (such as the mausoleums and crypts of New Orleans). The New Mexico Historic Preservation division recognizes the significance of the camposantos, but has not had the funds to systematically document them. Consequently a destroyed gravemarker is lost without any public record of its existence.

The question of preserving camposantos is raised by Susan Hazen-Hammond in a 1986 article.[5] She asks, "Is it really wise to try to freeze time and conserve the camposantos for the future just as they are now?

Or should the traditional pattern continue with nature, time, and changing customs all taking their toll?" To insist on preservation of the camposantos' existing qualities would put an end to their value as cultural indicators. Yet the loss of such highly personal, meaningful traditions would be lamentable.

Fortunately, there are still several hundred rural camposantos where change takes place more slowly, and perhaps the best we can do is to recognize and document these jewels in the landscape. The camposanto itself is a landscape that will be carried in the minds of those who see it. For those who witness the dramatic melding of land and people, for those who see the tiny stuffed bear tied with ribbons to little Maria's wooden cross, or the eyes of Reyes as he stares from his picture across the field of saints, there will be no forgetting this sacred place.

Mountain-side camposanto, Truchas

Laura Sue Sanborn

ADDENDUM

Particularly interesting markers may be found in these New Mexican villages:

Abiquiu	Chimayo	Madrid
Acoma	Cedar Crest	Mesilla
Albuquerque	Cordova	Placitas
Arroyo Hondo	Cuba	Ranchos de Taos
Belen	Escabosa	Santa Fe
Bernal	Espanola	San Ysidro
Bernalillo	Golden	Socorro
Capitan	La Cienega	Taos
Carrizozo	Lamy	Tesuque
Cebolla	Las Cruces	Tijeras
Cerrillos	Las Vegas	Tojique
Chilili	Los Lunas	Torreon

Special note should be taken of camposantos at Galisteo, Peralta, Tecolote, and Truchas. At White Oaks there is an interesting old Anglo cemetery.

NOTES

1. Terry G. Jordan, *Texas Graveyards; A Cultural Legacy* (Austin, Texas: University of Texas Press, 1982), 80.

2. Ibid., 112.

3. John R. Stilgoe, "Folklore and Graveyard Design", *Landscape*, (1978), 3:22.

4. Susan Hazen-Hammond, 1986. "Dios da y Dios quita", *New Mexico Magazine*, (1986), 7:64.

5. Ibid.

Fig. 1   Presenting Hand reaching downwards to a circular chain. Caroline Bieth, 1871, Preston Cemetery, Cambridge, Waterloo County.

UNITED ABOVE THOUGH PARTED BELOW: THE HAND AS SYMBOL ON NINETEENTH-CENTURY SOUTHWEST ONTARIO GRAVESTONES

Nancy-Lou Patterson

The white marble gravestones which characterize nineteenth-century graveyards in Southern Ontario have been remarked upon by several Canadian scholars.[1] Such markers were first produced in local workshops in the 1830s and have been called "distinctly Ontario stones," though in fact they are carved from imported calcite and strongly resemble stones found elsewhere in North America during the same period.[2]

The characteristic motifs which were used to adorn these marble stones include the willows and urns of Classical Revival symbolism, hands, animals such as birds and lambs, human figures and angels, flowers, and "miscellaneous" objects such as crosses, Bibles, and anchors.[3] The largest group is devoted to willow trees and the second largest to hands.[4] In Carole Hanks's study, *Early Ontario Gravestones*, some forty white marble stones are depicted; fifteen of these bear willows and ten bear hands. The willow motif has been successfully interpreted.[5] It is my intention to attempt an interpretation of the hand motifs.

United Above Though Parted Below

One might perceive stones with the hand motif as merely repetitive and banal, but close study reveals the variety and even richness of these forms. Their general meaning can be found in the stone from which I take my title (Fig. 1). This marker, which is a memorial to Caroline Bieth (1871) in Preston Cemetery, Cambridge, Ontario, in the southern part of the regional municipality of Waterloo, displays a descending hand, the forefinger of which is thrust down to close the links of a circular chain. The motto, carved in English on a stone otherwise inscribed in German, is

"United Above Though Parted Below." Implicit in these words is my thesis that all gravestone hand motifs express a relationship between the living and the dead. Such motifs present a double spatial symbolism, "Above" and "Below," combined with a binary structure of unified opposites, "United . . . Though Parted." This symbolic organization may be shown thus:

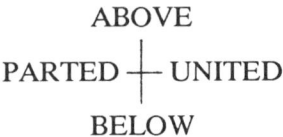

This motto presents in words the various meanings implicit in all hand gestures used in a mortuary setting.

The division of the world into a below and an above is deeply seated in human culture and certainly predates Christianity.[6] The vertical slab-shaped gravemarker is intended to be faced by a standing viewer, and the motifs are placed in relationship to a vertical dimension which expresses the above-below polarity, while the horizontal dimension expresses the "I-Thou" relationship between living and dead.

The orientational element in gravemarkers derives in Western culture through Classical culture from Mesopotamia, where the "cosmological symbolism of architecture [attained] . . . its richest development."[7] This symbolic structure was still fully operative in the popular culture of the Victorian era. Biblical language describing the ascension of Christ into Heaven and creedal language about His descent into hell to save souls were still strongly functional.

Geographical Areas of Research

My analysis of hand motifs will consider eighty stones garnered from thirty cemeteries. I have selected two areas of settlement.[8] The first is the Waterloo county heartland of Southwestern Ontario, which lies about eighty miles north of Lake Erie between Detroit on the west and Buffalo on the east; the second is the Bruce County area about 80-150 miles north of this region, located below the base of the Bruce Peninsula between Lake Huron and Georgian Bay, to its northern tip. Some of the settlers who came to the first region later moved north to create the second.

In southern Ontario, which in the late eighteenth and early nineteenth century was known as Upper Canada, and in the mid-nineteenth century as Canada West, settlement by whites began in the 1780s. Though French traders had been in the area since the early seventeenth century, the first settlers were mostly Loyalists from the upper states, including Pennsylvania, New York and New England. The early Loyalists of British descent settled along the Canadian shores of Lake Ontario from Kingston (near the head of the St. Lawrence River, north of New York State) to the Niagara Peninsula (near Niagara Falls and Buffalo, New York). It is in these areas that eighteenth-century gravestones can be found.

The Loyalists were followed by other settlers who came directly from Britain throughout the nineteenth century. These included English, Scottish, and Irish settlers, both Protestant and Roman Catholic. It was the Loyalist and British culture, during Victoria's reign (1837-1901), which formed the major influence upon commercial and popular culture in nineteenth-century English-speaking Canada, and which has determined the choice of motifs on most of the marble stones of my study.

This idea can be treated in Waterloo and Bruce Counties because both of these regions contained, in addition to those of Loyalist/British stock, substantial populations of German-speaking settlers. Settlement in Waterloo County began at the opening of the nineteenth century with

Mennonites and related Anabaptists from Pennsylvania, following their earlier arrival in the Niagara Peninsula in 1786. The cemeteries of these settlers and their descendants contain three time-related groups of stones: sandstone slabs (circa 1820-1850); marble slabs (circa 1840-1920), and granite stones of various shapes (circa 1890-present). With slight exception, only the sandstone markers of the Mennonites contain Pennsylvania-German elements, such as the lily/tulip.[9]

The second wave of Germanic settlement in Waterloo County was formed by Amish people direct from Alsace (circa 1825). Most of these settlers assimilated to Mennonite culture and through them to "Ontario culture," and their cemeteries contain, for the most part, the marble and subsequent granite stones described above. There were additional Amish settlers in Southern Ontario later in the nineteenth century who came from Pennsylvania, and a few of these groups have developed distinctive gravemarkers in the twentieth century.[10]

In the 1840s South German and Alsatian Roman Catholics, whose cemeteries also contain marble and granite (but not sandstone), together with many beautiful crosses of wrought iron and cast iron, came to the periphery of the Waterloo Region.[11] Members of these communities travelled north and settled in Bruce County in the 1860s. Both areas contain stones with Roman Catholic motifs such as crucifixes and sacred hearts, as well as motifs typical of the Ontario style. Other German-speaking people, including Pennsylvania Lutherans, who came to Waterloo County in the 1840s and some of whom moved north to Bruce County, also became assimilated and adopted the same style of gravemarkers.

As a result of these various settlement patterns, Waterloo and Bruce Counties contain stones of a larger number of both Pennsylvania and continental German-speaking people than do most other parts of Ontario, with the exception of Renfrew County. The predominant population in the nineteenth century in Southern Ontario was of Loyalist or British origin, and the inclusion of a few cemeteries from Wellington and Perth Counties, both adjacent to Waterloo County, allows a larger sample of these English-speaking settlements.

It is my finding that all of the above groups -- English- and German-speaking alike, as well as Roman Catholic, Lutheran, Mennonite, Amish, Presbyterian and United Church, used the white marble stones and included a similar range of hand motifs. My conclusion is that hand motifs are indeed ubiquitous and were widely accepted by all the ethnic and religious groups whose cemeteries are included in this study.

Time Distribution of Research

The eighty stones bearing hand motifs can be divided into three categories: those which display *linked hands*; those which show *upward pointing hands*; and those which bear *presenting hands*. I shall discuss each category in turn, but first I shall describe the time distribution of the stones.

Despite the degraded condition of some of the epitaphs, enough dates remain readable to allow an analysis of the time distribution of the categories of hand motif. The sequence of dateable Linked Hands includes thirty stones, which, taking all the sub-variations of this category together, are found from 1866 to 1928, a period of over sixty years. The distribution of all dated Linked Hand motifs is as follows: two stones from the 1860s, four from the 1870s, nine from the 1880s, and nine from the 1890s, three from the first decade of the twentieth century, two from the second, and one from the third. This forms a curve consonant with the development and decline of a style which was at its height during the two decades at the end of the nineteenth century. The Linked Hands motif is not only the most numerous and longest lasting hand motif but is also truly ubiquitous: all the cemeteries in my sample contain this motif.

The second most common motif, that of the Upward-pointing Hand, with twenty-one dateable stones, is found from 1855 to 1906 (fifty years), and is relatively equally represented in each of the five decades in which it appears, although there is still a discernible curve. The dated sequence begins with a single stone in 1855, progresses through six stones in the 1860s, four in the 1870s, four in the 1880s, three in the 1890s, and three in the first decade of the twentieth century. There is some evidence here of a stronger early preference for this motif tempered by a gradual decline.

Of the eleven dateable stones with Presenting Hands, which appear in a sequence from 1871 to 1900 (twenty-nine years), three are found in the 1870s, three in the 1880s, and five from 1893 to 1900. While not as popular as the Linked and Upward-pointing Hands, this motif is consistently found during the last three decades of the nineteenth century in my sample. In the following three sections I shall discuss each category in turn.

Linked Hands

The motif of a pair of hands which grasp one another in a handsclasp or handshake is used in thirty-five of the eighty stones of my sample. There are four variations of this longest lasting and most widely distributed motif.

The first and most common, with twenty stones, shows an open hand with all fingers extended, entering from the viewer's left, which is grasped by a hand entering from the viewer's right, of which the forefinger alone is extended, and the other three fingers are closed or clasped (Fig. 2). One senses that the first hand is very loose or limp and that the hand which clasps it does so in a rather formal or artificial gesture.

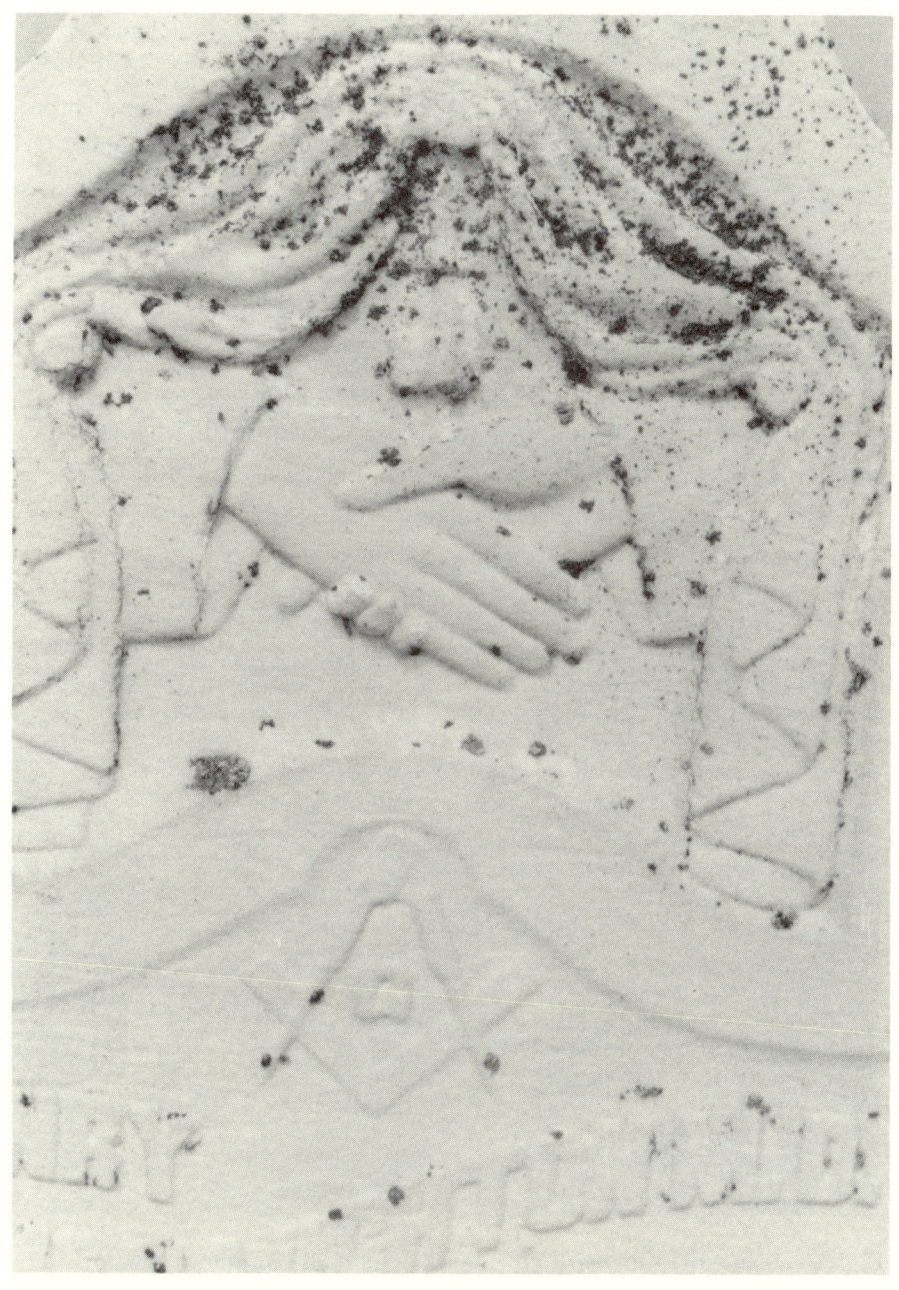

Fig. 2 Linked Hands with extended forefinger; detail of Henry McNaughton, 1896, Erin Cemetery, Erin, Wellington County.

The second variation, shown on seven stones, displays a hand with all four fingers extended being grasped very loosely by a second hand, which is also open with all four fingers extended (Fig. 3). Here the gesture is so loose as to be either feeble or entirely formalized, a mere laying of palm to palm, with only the thumb of the second hand pressing the knuckles of the first in a limp farewell. Yet the two crossed hands form a strong X-shaped motif which fills the visual field with vigorous diagonals.

In contrast, the third variation, found in six samples, shows an open hand entering from the left and grasped by a hand with all four fingers closed. This gives an impression of a firm handsclasp but still leaves the hand which enters from the left apparently unresponsive (Fig. 4). It also leaves the lower left portion of the design field empty and presents the folded forefinger as unnaturally long.

Fig. 3 Linked Hands with all fingers extended. Unknown person, 1877, Allenford United Church, Allenford, Bruce County.

Fig. 4 Linked Hands with all fingers closed on clasping hand. William Proctor, 1878, Allenford United Church, Allenford, Bruce County.

Finally, as a fourth variation, there are two stones, possibly by the same carver, in St. Andrew's Presbyterian Cemetery located halfway between Shakespeare and Amulree, Ontario, in which both hands are shown with all four fingers of each hand closed upon the other in a gesture which depicts a realistic handshake (Fig. 5). I have found no other example of this variation, though it appears in settings outside the mortuary, as for example in symbols of agreement signified by a handshake.

The majority of the stones bearing Linked Hands do not display a motto above the rondel in which the motif appears, but of those which do (and are readable), the mottoes are these: "Farewell," used in seven stones, "In Memory Of," used on three stones, "Farewell Father," "Farewell . . . Mother," "Bruderlieve," "Our Father and Mother," and "Nearer my God to Thee."

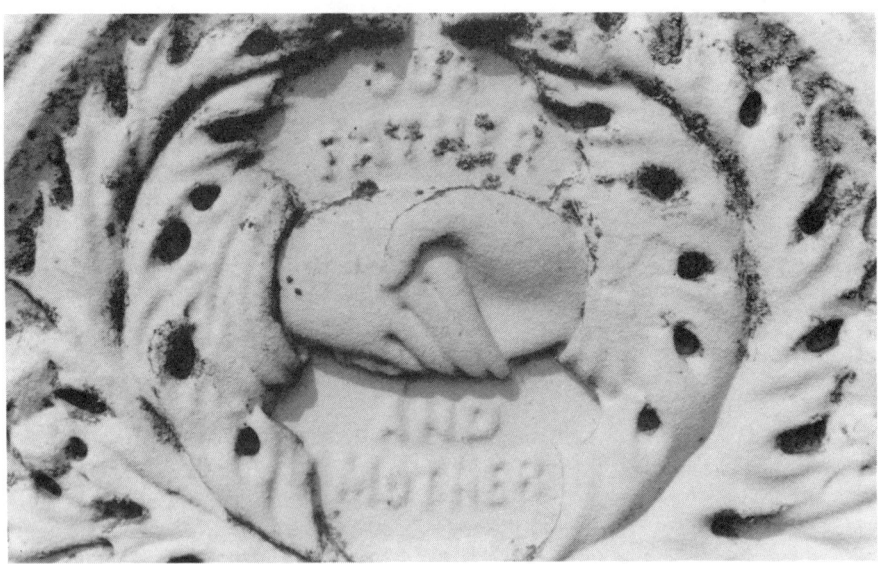

Fig. 5 Linked Hands with both hands fully closed; detail of Peter, c. 1872, and Catherine, 1892 McLellan, St. Andrew's Presbyterian Church Cemetery, located between Shakespeare and Amulree, Perth County.

This largest category of hand motifs is called by symbolist J.E. Cirlot "the familiar emblem of the 'linked hands'." He gives two interpretations of this gesture. The first is that it is "expressive of a virile fraternity." Barbara Franco's study of Masonic symbolism states that "clasped hands symbolize fidelity," and that in a fraternal context, they "symbolize giving and receiving signs of recognition."[12]

Since in Freemasonry it is the pressure of the thumb rather than the position of the fingers which is the sign, other motifs are necessary to suggest a fraternal interpretation for the Linked Hands. The stone of Henry McNaughton (1896) in Erin Cemetery, Erin, Ontario, Wellington County, (Fig. 2), displays a pair of Linked Hands above the square and compasses of Freemasonry. The stone of William A. Bryan (1893) in Rushes Cemetery, Crosshill, Ontario, Waterloo County, places the Linked Hands in the context of fraternal symbolism, where it is surrounded by a variety of Orange Lodge motifs, including the arch beneath which the hands appear.[13] A third stone, that of John Becker (1871), in Preston Cemetery, Cambridge, Ontario, Waterloo County, which also displays Linked Hands, has thrust into the earth before it a metal device bearing the triple linked chain and the letters "IOOF" which express membership in the International Order of Odd Fellows. In all of these stones the fraternal membership is made clear not by the Linked Hands but by additional and specifically lodge-related motifs.

Cirlot's second interpretation of the Linked Hands gesture is that it signifies "mystic marriage."[14] This is probably a more common meaning of the motifs in a mortuary setting, many of which appear on stones bearing epitaphs describing the dead as husband and/or wife. Very often the cuffs of the sleeves out of which the hands extend indicate the presence of male and female participants in the handclasp: a husband with a masculine, straight-edged shirt cuff, sometimes complete with a button or cuff-link;

and a wife with a feminine, ruffled or flaring cuff (Fig. 5). Gender is not indicated by the hands themselves, which are usually of the same size and shape, perhaps because there is no giving or taking in marriage in Heaven.

Another symbolist states that "clasping hands" signify "union" and "allegiance"," as well as friendship, loyalty, promise, agreement, contract, and confirmation.[15] These many generalized terms of mutuality and relationship reinforce the breadth and complexity of this motif. Its use continues to exist in the late twentieth century in this broad sense, but it appears very seldom in a mortuary setting beyond the Victorian and Edwardian eras, and then only on the marble stones.[16]

Linked Hands on a gravestone imply contact of the living and the dead not only at the moment of parting, or at the moment yet to come of greeting in another world, but also, in some mystical way, contact in the present. I argue this from the horizontal arrangement of the hands, which allows an analysis of the left-handedness or right-handedness of the hands depicted. In every case of the Linked Hands motifs examined in this study, the two hands are both right hands, and thus must be the hands of two different people, rather than the hands of a single person. It is notable that in nearly every case the hand entering from the left is shown with all four fingers extended in a limp manner. This person is evidently facing the viewer and presenting a right hand to the viewer, whose own right hand is inserted from the right side and actively grasps the hand of the other. If this is so, perhaps the hand entering from the left is the hand of the dead. There is nothing macabre in this contact of dead and living. The hands are extended from left and right in a position of equality. This symbol of greeting, when found on a tombstone, implies the hope of meeting the dead again, when the hands of both participants will be the hands of the dead, and not only the dead but the resurrected. Such a hope is suggested by the epitaph found on the stone of Janet, wife of Archibald Rennie, (1872) in Rushes Cemetery, Crosshill, Ontario, Waterloo County: "Farewell Till We Meet Again."

That the most common of hand motifs found on Victorian stones--the Linked Hands--can be carved in four different gestural manners, suggests that even for its carvers this was not the monotonous reiteration of a stereotype but a lively embodiment of that most desired of all meanings-- the contact through an image carved on stone between the one whose body lies in the earth and the one who stands before it ready to read that meaning anew.

Upward-Pointing Hands

In the second largest category of hand motifs are twenty-nine Upward-pointing Hands. These are clearly divided into two groups. The largest and most broadly distributed group includes twenty-two Upward-pointing Hands inside rondels, each placed at the top of its stone (Fig. 6). There are mottoes placed above this image in about half of these stones and some of these mottoes comment upon the direction taken by the dead as indicated by the upraised forefinger: "Gone Home" (used twice in Rushes Cemetery), "Gone Before," "Gone to Glory," and "To Heaven." Other mottoes comment upon the state of the dead: "She is at Rest," and "There is Rest in Heaven." One addresses God: "Thy will be done." An epitaph on the stone of Philippina, Wife of Adam Halberstadt, (1863) in Preston Cemetery, Cambridge, Ontario, summarizes the meaning of these mottoes very clearly:

> Jesus has called the mother home
> Her flesh lies mouldering in the ground:
> God grant her offspring may be blessed
> And meet her in eternal rest.

Fig. 6   Upward-pointing Hand; detail of Anna Wagner, 1889, St. Peter's Lutheran Cemetery, Neustadt, Bruce County.

The Upward-pointing Hand is found in other symbolic settings in nineteenth-century artifacts. A well-known example in Waterloo County is the handsome cast-iron Upward-pointing Hand which once topped the steeple of St. Paul's Lutheran Church in Bridgeport, Ontario (now part of Kitchener), Waterloo County. This object tops the steeple of the Freeport United Church in its own relocated position at Doon Heritage Crossroads, Kitchener, Ontario.[17] It shows the thumb and forefinger firmly pointed upwards and the other three fingers carefully folded downwards. A lightning rod has been fastened to the hand in case the steeple should attract fire from heaven. In this position on the church, as on the stones, the Upward-pointing Hand is part of the emblematic tradition which the Victorian era had perpetuated, and its purpose is to direct attention upwards, toward the symbolic location of Heaven.

This symbolism has been modified in the late twentieth century by emphasis on the singularity of the raised forefinger. In the 1980s athletes (and their fans) raise their forefingers to signal that they are "number one." That is, they are the first in their class and have reached the top of their group. Even here the gesture is associated with victory. There is a sense in which the element of victory is included when the same gesture is used in a mortuary setting as an image of transcendence, and in particular, of victory over death.

The gesture of the Upward-pointing Hand as used in the nineteenth century may be derived from the depiction of angels at the tomb of Christ who point upward to tell the mourning women on Easter that Christ has risen from the dead, or of angels who, at the ascension of Christ into Heaven, point upwards to tell the assembled followers of Jesus that He will return even as they have seen Him go. Sunday school booklets of this period often show these scenes.

When hands on gravestones point upwards without a visual referent, there is a suggestion that it is some angelic or otherwise lofty commentator who points, signalling to the viewer the direction taken by the departed. Sometimes, however, there *is* a visual referent plainly indicated. This situation forms a secondary category of Upward-pointing Hands on seven stones found in St. Boniface Roman Catholic Cemetery in Maryhill, Ontario, Waterloo County, and in St. Peter's Lutheran Cemetery in Neustadt, Ontario, Bruce County. It may be that these stones in which the Upward-pointing Hand is directed toward a visible target comprise a distinctive variation or exception in that they possess a denominational, ethnic, or carver-related element confined to these sites.

In St. Peter's Lutheran Cemetery, Neustadt, Ontario, Bruce County, one stone shows an Upward-pointing Hand in a small rondel beneath a large rondel containing an open Bible. This target (the Bible) is unique in this series. A stone in the Neustadt cemetery (1894) places the hand in a rondel beneath a larger rondel which contains as its target the Cross bearing the initials "IHS" (a Greek symbol for Jesus, derived from the spelling of His name in Greek capitals, and sometimes explained as standing for standing for the Latin *Jesus Hominum Salvator*) and flanked by lilies. These stones are very similar in format and shape, but the date on the one with the Bible is entirely concealed by lichen.

In St. Boniface Cemetery, Maryhill, there are five stones with Upward-pointing Hands indicating the Cross as its target. One of these, with a hand in a rondel pointing up to a rondel containing a Cross flanked by lilies and with an IHS looks very much like the 1894 stone in Neustadt and bears a date of 1895. There are slight differences in the presentation of the details, but both the Neustadt and Maryhill stones are lettered in German gothic script. In Maryhill there is another stone with a hand in a vertical ellipse pointing up toward a lily-flanked Cross with the IHS in a circular rondel; here the date is 1891 and the lettering is in English script. These three stones are enough alike to suggest that they were done by the same carver or have a common design source.

A third stone at Maryhill, which is broken and undateable, contains a wreath-enclosed Upward-pointing Hand in a large rondel beneath a Cross with an IHS inside a small rondel without flowers. This can be classed with those discussed above as to theme, but there are significant variations in the presentation. Also at Maryhill are two stones in which the Upward-pointing Hand, enclosed in a vertical ellipse, is deeply set within the arms of a large Cross surmounting the stone. One such Cross bears the IHS and the other bears three trefoils, one on each arm of the Cross. Each stone places the Cross above a rondel containing a rose bouquet. Both stones are lettered in German gothic; one of these stones is dated 1868 and was made in Elora. Carvers of this type of stone placed their names and business locations near the base of the stone, and this information is very often unreadable.

All these Hands direct attention not only to Heaven, but to the Bible or the Cross, that is, to the source of consolation and instrument of salvation by which Heaven has been won for the dead. In all these cases, moreover, the hand is in a distinct rondel of its own, whether it is placed beneath a separate rondel containing the Bible or Cross, or is placed upon the Cross.

A final stone in this thematic set, that of Alexander Miller (1860), is distinctly different in format but seems to have the same meaning, expressed even more emphatically and clearly (Fig. 7). In this stone a hand appears to burst forth from the earth beside a Cross raised on a set of stairs, and obviously the hand points toward the Cross. Here, too, the letters IHS are prominently displayed. This hand is perhaps the hand of the buried dead, pointing firmly toward the Cross in which the hopes of the living and the dead are to be placed.

Presenting Hands

The third and last major category of hand motifs appears on sixteen stones; I shall call these motifs Presenting Hands. All of them hold or present an object up, down, or out to the viewer's attention. More than half of those (eleven) lift an object upwards: that is, the hand reaches up from below, as does the Upward-pointing Hand, and holds or presents an object in the upheld hand (Fig. 8). A few of these hands hold up nosegays or bouquets of flowers, many hold up open Bibles, and one, in St. Peter's Lutheran Cemetery in Neustadt, Ontario, holds a heart in its open palm. The same cemetery contains an Upward-pointing Hand which clasps a fistful of leaves, unique in the works studied.

In Rushes Cemetery near Crosshill, Ontario, there are five stones with upheld Bibles with the motto "REV. XIV:13," referring to a long verse, *Revelation* 14:13, the meat of which is the phrase "Blessed are the dead which die in the Lord." A stone bearing an upheld Bible in Erin, Ontario, Wellington County, bears the motto "God is Love." There are several

Fig. 7   Upward-pointing Hand directed toward a Cross.   Alexander Miller, 1860, St. Boniface Roman Catholic Church, Maryhill, Waterloo County.

Fig. 8   Presenting Hand uplifting an open Bible. Elizabeth Armstrong, 1888, Rushes Cemetery, near Crosshill, Waterloo County.

other upheld Bible stones with mottoes which I was unable to decipher because of their worn condition. The space on the Bible page is small and the lettering small and shallow, so that these messages are easily worn away.

The next, and with only four examples, much smaller group of Presenting Hands, includes four which reach downward from above, holding objects which hang down or are touched from above (Fig. 1). On each of two of these stones a downward-reaching hand is presenting a scroll to the viewer's attention. On one of these, the stone of Sally Hagey (1895) in Hagey Cemetery, Cambridge, Ontario, Waterloo County, the scroll bears the motto "At Rest."

On a stone in Dunk's Bay Cemetery, Tobermorey, Ontario, in Bruce County, located at the northern tip of the Bruce Peninsula, a funerary drape is pulled aside by rosettes to reveal a downward-reaching Presenting Hand holding a large escutcheon on a cord, with a nosegay of three roses between the dependent cord's two portions. In memory of Alexander Butchard (1892), the epitaph of this elaborately detailed stone declares, "Too good for earth, / God called him home."

The last of the downward Presenting Hands carries the motto from which the title of this article was taken. Here a hand reaches down with its forefinger extended, holding together two links of a circular chain (Fig. 1). A severed chain, in which the links of the circle have been broken by death, here becomes a reunited chain in which, by divine intervention, the circle becomes unbroken once again. This hand, it seems to me, is indeed the hand of God, and it is the dead woman and her mourners who are to be "United Above Though Parted Below."

Finally, there is a single stone in my samples with a Presenting Hand which reaches sideways, entering the visual field from the viewer's right and extending a nosegay (Fig. 9). This posture apparently lacks the reference to Heaven and suggests the offering of a floral tribute to a child,

Willie S. Martin, who died in 1890 at the age of seven years. There is, however, a heavenly reference in the poignant epitaph lettered below: "You are gone little Willie ... To stately mansions above."

Fig. 9   Presenting Hand extending a bouquet from the side. Willie S. Martin, 1890, Grace United Church, Millbank, Waterloo County.

In the category of Presenting Hands I have described three directional variations: the rising (or raising) hand, the descending hand, and the horizontal hand. This directionality can be interpreted in accordance with the idea of a three-storey universe. The descending Presentational Hand suggests, by its spatial association with the "Hand of God," the giving of a gift or the bringing of a message, or even the direct intervention from the spiritual realm, that is, from Heaven. The horizontal Presentational Hand suggests an offering from within the living world in the viewer's own plane, as does its accompanying epitaph which addresses the dead in the voice perhaps of the bereaved parents. The rising Presentational Hand, however, like the far more common Upward-pointing Hand, surely does not suggest an infernal manifestation but rather an effort to lift or direct upwards the attention of the viewer, elevating or raising the thoughts of the onlooker from the earthly to the heavenly.

In the extremely archaic and psychologically powerful multilayered universe which was still occupied by the people who raised these marble stones with their ubiquitous hand motifs, the hands implied a continuum of being, and even of interaction, between the below and the above, between the living and the dead, and between the human and the divine. The hand is the prime symbol of personal action and direct efficacy. In this symbol the worlds of the person whose death is memorialized on the stone, of the bereaved survivors who anticipated a heavenly reunion with the departed, and even of the passerby who pauses to view and perhaps to reflect upon the meaning of that stone, are, at least for a moment, united.

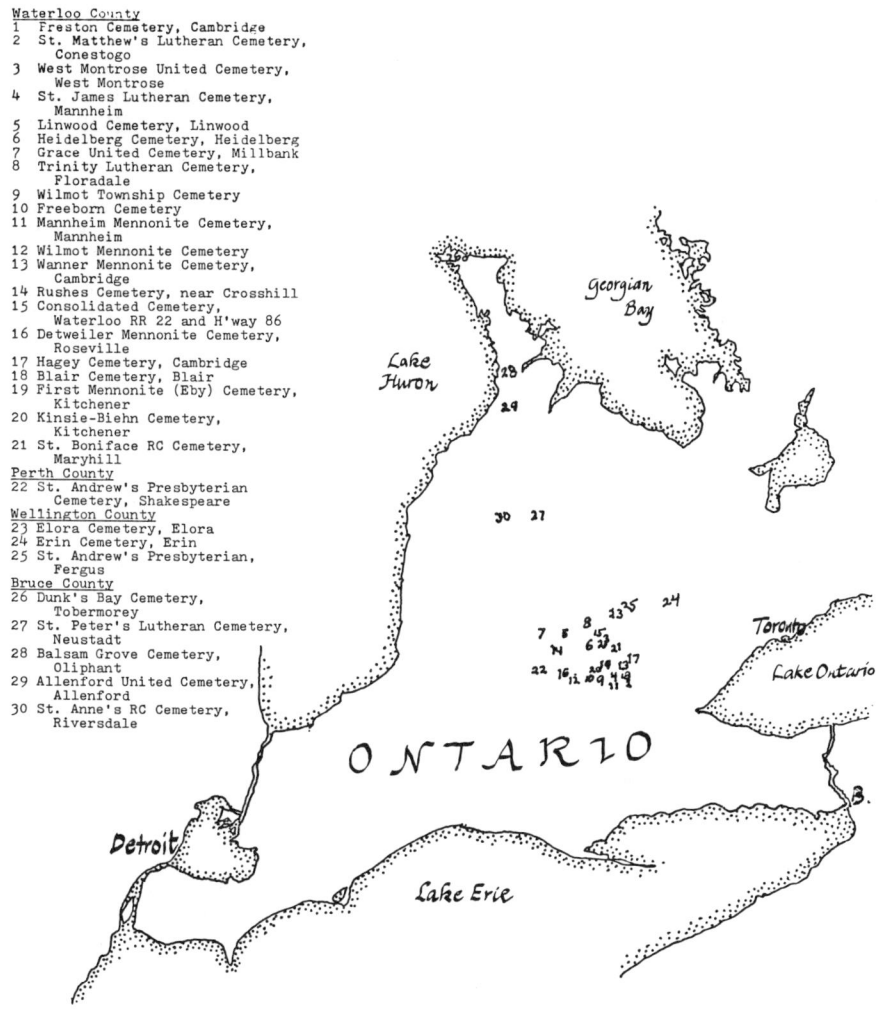

Map of Southwestern Ontario, indicating cemeteries visited.

Nancy-Lou Patterson

NOTES

All photographs are by the author.

1. Carole Hanks, *Early Ontario Gravestones* (Toronto: McGraw-Hill Ryerson, 1974); and Patricia Stone and Lynn Russell, "Observations on Figures, Human and Divine, on Nineteenth Century Ontario Gravestones," *Material History Bulletin* (Fall 1986), 23-30.

2. Stone and Russell, "Observations," 23. An advertisement for cabinetmaker and stonecutter Johannes Hoffman (1808-1878) featuring two gravestones and a willow tree appeared in *Der Deutsche Canadier* (28 February 1839) in Berlin (now Kitchener), Ontario. This is reproduced in Teruko Kobayashi, "Folk Art in Stone: Pennsylvania German Gravemarkers in Ontario," *Waterloo Historical Society Annual Volume 1982* (Kitchener, Ontario: Waterloo Historical Society, 1983), 70:111. The Waterloo County gravestones are cut from imported calcite (a metamorphosed limestone commonly used as marble) according to tests done by Professor R. Gwylim Roberts of the Department of Earth Sciences at the University of Waterloo (Ontario), whose help is gratefully acknowledged.

3. Hanks, *Early Ontario Gravestones*, 32; and Stone and Russell "Observations," 23. Willow and hand motifs occur commonly in Victoria era stones in the United States as well; see Francis Y. Duval and Ivan B. Rigby, *Early American Gravestone Art in Photographs* (New York: Dover Publications, 1978), 108-109 and 111-115 for willow motifs in Iowa cemeteries; for hands see Duval and Rigby 118, 120, 122, 125; and Edmund V. Gillon Jr., *Victorian Cemetery Art* (New York: Dover Publications, 1972), figs. 58-59, 124-127 and 129-130.

4. Hanks, *Early Ontario Gravestones*, 35; Stone and Russell, "Observations," 23.

5. Blanche M.G. Linden, "The Willow Tree and Urn Motif: Changing Ideas about Death and Nature," *Markers I* (Worcester, MA: AGS Publications, 1979-1980), 149-155. Willows were widely used in Victorian funerary symbolism; see Barbara Jones, *Design for Death* (London: Andre Deutsch, 1967) for mid-nineteenth century British printers' blanks for funeral cards with willow trees (137) and a mid-nineteenth century British catalogue of printers' stock blocks for undertakers' and masons' cards with a series of willow motifs. See also footnote 3 above.

6. Just as ceremonial burial itself developed in the Paleolithic Age [see Mircea Eliade, *A History of Religious Ideas*, Volume I (Chicago: University of Chicago Press, 1987), "Symbolic Meanings of Burials," 9-13], so also did the concept of a vertical orientation of space as a cosmic model, analogous to the upright posture of human beings. Eliade calls this "the original and originating experience" which separates humans from pre-humans" (Ibid., 3).

7. Ibid., 43

8. The cemeteries are as follows: *Waterloo County*: Preston Cemetery, Cambridge, Ontario; St. Matthew's Evangelical Lutheran Cemetery, Conestoga, Ontario; West Montrose United Church cemetery, West Montrose, Ontario; St. James Evangelical Lutheran Cemetery, Mannheim, Ontario; Linwood Cemetery, Linwood, Ontario; Heidelberg Cemetery, Heidelberg, Ontario; Grace United Church, Millbank, Ontario; Trinity Lutheran Church, Floradale, Ontario; Wilmot Township Senior Public School Cemetery; Freeborn Cemetery, Wellesley Township; Mannheim Mennonite Church Cemetery, Mannheim, Ontario; Wilmot Mennonite Church Cemetery, Wilmot Township; Wanner Cemetery (Wanner Mennonite Church), Cambridge, Ontario; Rushes Cemetery, near Crosshill, Ontario; Consolidated Cemetery, Waterloo Regional Road 22 and Highway 86; Detweiler Mennonite Meeting House, Roseville, Ontario; Hagey Cemetery, Cambridge, Ontario; Blair Cemetery, Blair, Ontario; First Mennonite (Eby) Church Cemetery, Kitchener, Ontario; Kinsie-Biehn Cemetery, Kitchener, Ontario; St. Boniface Roman Catholic Cemetery, Maryhill, Ontario; *Perth County*: St. Andrew's Presbyterian Churh, Shakespeare-Amulree, Ontario; *Wellington County*: Elora Cemetery, Elora, Ontario; Erin Cemetery, Erin, Ontario; St. Andrew's Presbyterian Cemetery, Fergus, Ontario; *Bruce County*: Dunk's Bay Cemetery, Tobermorey, Ontario; St. Peter's Lutheran Cemetery, Neustadt, Ontario; Balsam Grove Cemetery, Oliphant, Ontario; Allenford United Church Cemetery, Allenford, Ontario; St. Anne's Roman Catholic Church Cemetery, Riversdale, Ontario.

9. See Nancy-Lou Patterson, "Grave Matters: Swiss-German Mennonite Gravestones of the 'Pennsylvania Style' (1804-1854) in the Waterloo Region, Ontario," *Past and Present* (a University of Waterloo Periodical, October 1980), 56; "Death and Ethnicity: Swiss-German Mennonite Gravestones of the 'Pennsylvania Style' (1804-1854) in the Waterloo Region, Ontario," *Mennonite Life* (September 1982), Vol. 37, No. 3, 4-7; and "Swiss-German Mennonite Gravestones of the 'Pennsylvania Style' (1804-1854)," *Newsletter of the Association For Gravestone Studies* (Winter 1983/84), 4. For the exceptions, which consist of three white marble stones found in First Mennonite (Eby) Cemetery, Kitchener, Ontario, that appear to bear inscriptions based upon the *fraktur* lettering style of Isaac Z. Hunsicker, see Nancy-Lou Patterson, *Handschriften: Handwritten Forms in Germanic Waterloo County* (Kitchener, Ontario: Joseph Schneider Haus, 1984), Figure 7: Gravemarker for Magdalena Hunsicker (1854).

10. See Nancy-Lou Patterson, *Wreath and Bough: Decorative Arts of the Amish-Mennonite Settlers in Waterloo County* (Waterloo, Ontario: Ontario German Folklife Society, 1983), Figure 19 and p. 11; and *Handschriften* (1984), Figure 11. These distinctive gravemarkers are slabs of cast concrete inscribed with a pointed instrument in a naive "public school" script.

11. See Nancy-Lou Patterson, "The Iron Cross and the Tree of Life: German-Alsatian Gravemarkers in Waterloo Region and Bruce County Roman Catholic Cemeteries," *Ontario History* (March 1976), 1-16; "German-Alsatian Gravemarks in Ontario," *Past*

and Present (October 1978), 56; and "German-Alsatian Iron Gravemrkers in Southern Ontario Roman Catholic Cemeteries," *Material History Bulletin* (Fall 1983), 2 pp, 2 illustrations.

12. J.E. Cirlot, *A Dictionary of Symbols* (New York: American Philosophical Society, 1962), 131; and Barbara Franco, *Masonic Symbols in American Decorative Arts* (Lexington, Massachusetts: Scottish Rite Masonic Museum of Our National Heritage, 1976), 50.

13. This stone is illustrated in Nancy-Lou Patterson, "Be Thou Faithful Unto Death," *Past and Present* (October 1984), 6, and in "The Gavel of Death: Masonic and Orange Lodge Gravemarkers in Rushes Cemetery near Crosshill, Ontario (1864-1983), *Waterloo County Historical Society Annual Volume 1984* (Kitchener, Ontario: Waterloo Historical Society, 1985), 144.

14. Cirlot, *A Dictionary of Symbols*, 131.

15. J.C. Cooper, *Symbolism, the Universal Language* (Wellingborough, Northhamptonshire: The Aquarian Press, 1982), 117; and J.C. Cooper, *An Illustrated Encyclopedia of Traditional Symbols* (London: Thames and Hudson, 1978).

16. I have seen occasional examples in late twentieth-century stones of a hand motif not used in the stones studied in this paper: the Praying Hands motif, probably derived from the frequently reproduced Durer drawing, which I assume symbolizes prayer by the living for the dead.

17. Bridgeport Cemetery and Free Church were founded by the Rev. August Rauschenbush, who was born in 1816 in Altena, Westfalen, Germany, ordained a Lutheran pastor in 1841, and, having been given adult baptism in 1850, became a Baptist minister in 1851. He founded the first German Baptist Church in Canada, Benton Street Baptist Church in downtown Kitchener, Ontario, of which the Bridgeport Free Church was a branch. In 1861 German-speaking Lutherans in Bridgeport began to hold their services in this building, and did so until 1889, when St. Paul's Lutheran Church was erected, with its Upward-pointing Hand upon the spire. The cemetery continues in its original place. See Idessa Zimmerman, "Bridgeport, Ontario," (no date), a typescript. I am grateful to Elizabeth McNaughton, Registrar/Researcher of Doon Heritage Crossroads, for this information. The religious and ethnic elements represented in the history of the church which bears this symbol reflect the setting in which this particular Upward-pointing Hand was situated.

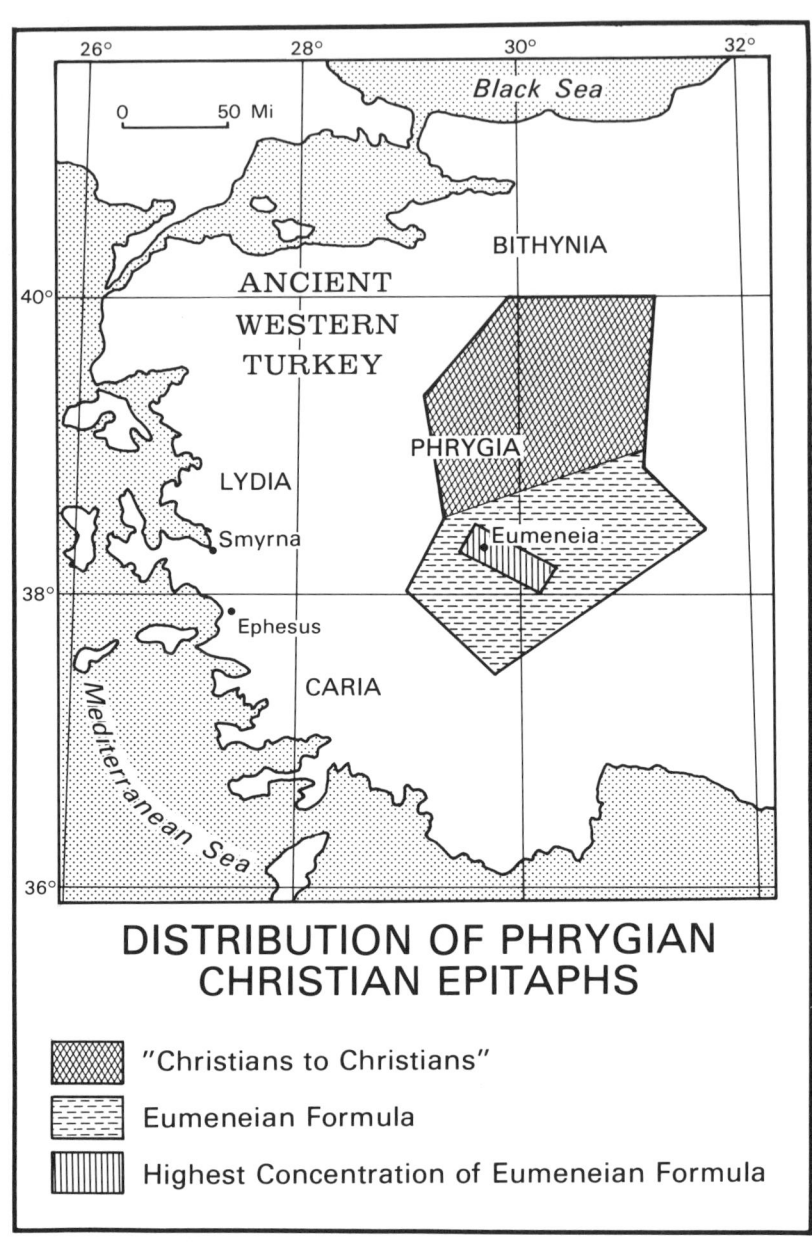

Map of Anatolia (*drawn by Carol Gerber*).

AN EARLY CHRISTIAN ATHLETE: THE EPITAPH OF AURELIUS EUTYCHUS OF EUMENEIA

Scott T. Carroll

Riches await the classical historian interested in tombstones. Ancient gravemarkers abound with fascinating material about the lives and professed beliefs of antiquity's "silent majority." There are thousands of extant tombstones inscribed in the native languages of the ancient Mediterranean world. Several excellent studies survey ancient Greek and Latin epigraphy.[1] The epitaphs of ancient Turkey (Anatolia, later known as Asia Minor) are thoroughly catalogued and are of particular interest.[2] The earliest epitaphic attestations to Christianity are found in the huge corpus of gravestones from Asia Minor. This paper describes one of them -- the tomb of Aurelius Eutychus. He was an athlete, and his nickname, Helix, meaning twisting or turning, probably applied to his skill as a wrestler. The inscription on the tomb provides an excellent example of syncretism -- the effort to reconcile or combine different religious beliefs, here paganism and Christianity.

Christianity was an illicit religion in the Roman Empire until its legalization by the Emperor Constantine in A. D. 313. This date marks a watershed in the study of early Christian epigraphy. After the Roman legalization of Christianity, except during the reign of Julian the Apostate (A.D. 361-363), it became fashionable to confess openly one's Christian faith on gravemarkers. Prior to the reign of Constantine, the church suffered through intermittent persecution. Believers in Asia Minor paid a heavy toll for their illegal faith. Funerary dedications that testified to Christianity before A.D. 313 jeopardized the well-being of Christians living in the vicinity of such unconventionally bold epitaphs. As a rule, an open profession of Christianity on tombstones was avoided prior to A.D.

313.³ The tombstones from pre-Constantine Asia Minor, where numerous epitaphs courageously placarded Christianity in the face of persecution, were an exception to this rule.

The earliest Christian epitaphs from Asia Minor are classified according to their formulae into two categories. The Christian epitaphs employed either an unveiled or a veiled formula. The unveiled formula is overtly Christian and boldly proclaims that the tomb was dedicated "by Christians for Christians" (Fig. 1).⁴ These epitaphs seemed to invite persecution. Twenty-four "Christians for Christians" tombstones have been found in eastern Lydia and west-central Phrygia (see map).

Divergent interpretations are offered to explain this unusual type of dedication. Several scholars maintain that these bold declarations of Christianity were made by Christian schismatics called Montanists.⁵ Montanism began in Phrygia in A.D. 171/2. The Montanists were prophetic, puritanical rigorists who called themselves "the Church of the martyrs." Their unhesitant proclamation of Christianity seemed to invite persecution. Montanism flourished in the region where the "Christians for Christians" epitaphs were erected. Other scholars are reluctant to identify the formula with the Montanists.⁶ Some attempt to account for the recurring epitaphic formula by arguing that the "Christians for Christians" gravestones were produced by the same workshop.⁷

Unlike the bold "Christians for Christians" epitaphs, the second category of pre-Constantine Christian dedications from Asia Minor are unobtrusive. The veiled formula was characterized by a syncretistic camouflage of the Christian testimony on the epitaph. These crypto-Christian inscriptions used imprecations and artistic motifs that were indistinguishable from those on pagan tombstones and consequently were inoffensive to their pagan neighbors. This kind of inscription contained a unique monotheistic dedication which has been positively identified as

Fig. 1 Early Christian tomb in Anatolia.

Christian.[8] The veiled inscription is called the "Eumeneian formula" because it is popularly attested around the Phrygian city of Eumeneia (see map).

The sepulchre had an important function in Phrygian society. The Phrygians believed that the grave was "the house of the dead." They employed elaborate precautions to protect their tombs against desecration by the interment of an unauthorized corpse. These precautions were often framed as legal proscriptions against violators of the tomb.[9] The stock proscription read: "If anyone disturbs this grave or buries an alien corpse in it, he shall pay a fine of so much to so and so." Apparently, these inscriptions were legally binding. Another common Phrygian proscription formula committed violators of the grave to a power higher than their courts -- to their gods. These types of inscription are called *devotiones*. The stock *devotiones* read: "The violator of this grave shall make an account to the gods." These two kinds of protection formulae were also employed by Phrygian Christians.

The Eumeneian formula incorporated dedication styles that discreetly hid Christian sentiments within the pagan epitaphial format. Utilizing the pagan invocations, the Christians declared their faith, using monotheistic references in an unobjectionable manner. For example, many Eumeneian Christian epitaphs read that the violator of the tomb should "pay before the true God." Other veiled Christian gravemarkers committed the protection of the tomb to "the Living God."

A veiled inscription that deserves observation because of its Christian confession and bold syncretism is the intriguing epitaph of Aurelius Eutychus of Eumeneia, called Helix.[10] His tombstone was located in Ishekli (ancient Eumeneia). The tribulations endured by Helix's headstone are a story in themselves. The gravestone was first observed in the masonry of a Turkish house on a road leading out of Ishekli. Ancient tombstones were frequently used to build walls, steps and even houses.

The inscription on the front of Helix's stone was copied in the late nineteenth century when it was observed in the wall of the house.[11] A Greek Christian force rampaged and burned Ishekli in 1922, and Helix's marker lay dislodged where the house once stood. The Muslims then protested the destruction of their town and desecrated Christian gravestones. Part of Helix's stone was mutilated. A team of epigraphists surveying the region later discovered, to their suprise, that Helix's gravemarker was inscribed on both the left and right sides. The interesting biographical information that had been hidden in the wall of the house was then recorded for the first time. The present location of the stone, if indeed it still exists, is unknown.

The altar-shaped stone was 0.72 meters high, 0.44 meters wide at the base and 0.305 meters wide along the shaft, with a thickness of 0.31 meters. The letters on the front of the headstone ranged in height from 2 to 1.8 centimeters, and the letters on the left side ranged in height from 1.3 to 1 centimeters (Figs. 2, 3 and 4).

The author's translation of the inscription is based on transcriptions published by Paris and Ramsay (see note 11):

> To the blessed dead. Aurelius Eutychus, son of Hermes, also called Helix, a Eumeneian citizen and a citizen of other cities, of the tribe of Hadrianis, a member of the city council and of the board of elders, made the grave for himself and his most reverend and dearest wife Marcella and their children. And if anyone else shall attempt to lay a corpse in it, he shall have to reckon with the Living God.

Fig. 2 Front of Eutychus marker.

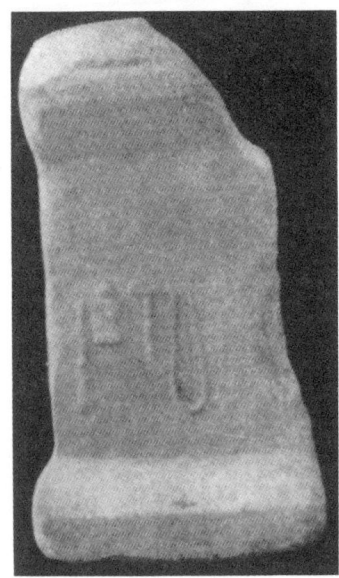

Fig. 3 Right side of Eutychus marker.

Fig. 4 Left side of Eutychus marker.

Since Helix's inscription is dateless, it is of primary importance to fix the date of the epitaph. There are several ways to establish the date of an undated epitaph. First, the date of an inscription can be approximated by the style of lettering and indications of contemporary pronunciation. The square sigmas used on the lettering were a stylistic idyosyncracy dating to the mid- third century A.D.[12]

Second, dating the formula used on a gravemarker is another convention employed to fix the date of a tombstone. Helix used the Eumeneian formula in his dedication. His inscription reads, "And if anyone else shall attempt to lay a corpse in this grave, he shall have to reckon with the Living God." This formula is pre-Constantine, dating to the last half of the third century. Scholars believe that the Eumeneian formula was intentionally designed to parallel the more overtly Christian epitaphic testimonials to the north of Eumeneia. All of the "Christians for Christians" inscriptions, with the exception of one, are dated between A.D. 246-73, suggesting that the Eumeneian formula was also popularly used at the same time.[13]

A third technique used to date such a monument is to analyze evidence that can be dated within the dedication. The presence of the name "Aurelius" places the date of the inscription after A.D. 212, when the Emperor Caracalla issued the *Constitutio Antoniniana*, which awarded Roman citizenship to all free inhabitants in the Roman Empire.[14] Aurelius became the *nomen* of the new Roman citizens during the third century, commemorating Caracalla's edict. Epitaphs with the *nomen* "Aurelius" are safely dated between A.D. 215 and A.D. 300. Helix's tombstone may be confidently dated between A.D. 250-300 by these criteria.

Along with the new privilege of citizenship extended to the family of Aurelius Eutychus came the obligation to participate in the imperial cult. It was especially during the third century A.D. that the Romans revived the state religion, obligating all citizens to participate in mandatory oblations to honor the genius of the emperor. Christians who refused to sacrifice faced the threat of imprisonment and death.[15] Christian persecution in the third century was especially intense during the reign of Decius (A.D. 249-51) and certainly during the lifetime of Aurelius Eutychus. Helix's *nomen* is a reminder of the conflict that faced this Eumeneian Christian, and it underscores the boldness of his epitaph, which was dedicated in the midst of persecution.

The other names on the gravestone are also of interest. The name Eutychus, literally meaning "good fortune," is commonly found on Christian and pagan tombstones alike.[16] It is not unusual for the name of the Greek god Hermes to be found in a Christian epitaph, as witnessed by other Christian epitaphs from Eumeneia.[17] Helix's father's parents were probably not Christians when they named their son "Hermes." Consequently, it is likely that Aurelius was a second, or if he was himself a convert, a first, generation Christian.

Helix's wife was named Marcella. She was probably raised in a home with Christian ancestry. The name Marcella was a derivative of the name of a prominent Phrygian Christian family from the late second century. Aviricius Marcellus (St. Abericius) was a Bishop in the Phrygian city of Hierapolis (see map) from A.D. 180-200).[18] Aviricius Marcellus has one of the most celebrated Christian epitaphs from Asia Minor. His gravestone bears the earliest positively identifiable Christian epitaph in Asia Minor. Aviricius Marcellus's epitaphic formula and legend made a profound impact on later Phrygian Christianity. It appears therefore that Helix married a woman from a Christian family who was named after this eminent Phrygian saint. Finally, the epithet declaring his wife "most reverend and dearest" is characteristically Christian and underscores the devotion that Helix had for Marcella.

As the text on the stone clearly indicates, Aurelius Eutychus composed his own epitaph and has consequently left for antiquity some interesting data about his occupation and activities.[19] A poker, anvil, hammer, and tongs were inscribed on the right side of the tombstone (Fig. 4), showing that Aurelius was a blacksmith. A common method of indicating the occupation of the deceased in antiquity was by inscribing the tools of his trade on his tombstone.[20] Several illustrations demonstrate that these tools were peculiar to the occupation of the smith. Hephaestus, the mythological blacksmith of the Olympian gods, was depicted on a Phrygian coin from Temenothyrae with a hammer, tongs, and anvil.[21] There is also a relief of a blacksmith holding tongs over an anvil from Asia Minor[22] and another tomb from the vicinity of Helix's gravemarker with a blacksmith's implements inscribed on it.[23] One of the clearest depictions of the smith's tools is on a Roman sarcophagus from a tomb in Ostia (Fig. 5).[24] The Roman writer Lucian even described the plight of a blacksmith's widow who was compelled to sell her husband's hammer, tongs, and anvil.[25] Aurelius Eutychus was certainly a member of a local smith's trade guild which was likely to have been organized in honor of their patron god Hephaestus. This kind of association was unavoidable for the early Christians and does not necessarily imply that there was participation in any cultic activity.

The Christian blacksmith from Eumeneia was also an athlete. The deceased's athletic career is indicated by several details on his tombstone. "Helix" was a common honorific nickname given to athletes. Additional evidence of Helix's involvement in athletics was inscribed on the side of the gravestone. An oil vase, two strigils, a pair of boxing gloves, and three crowns with palms appear on the left side of Helix's tombstone (Fig. 4).

Fig. 5 Roman sarcophagus from Ostia showing smith's tools.

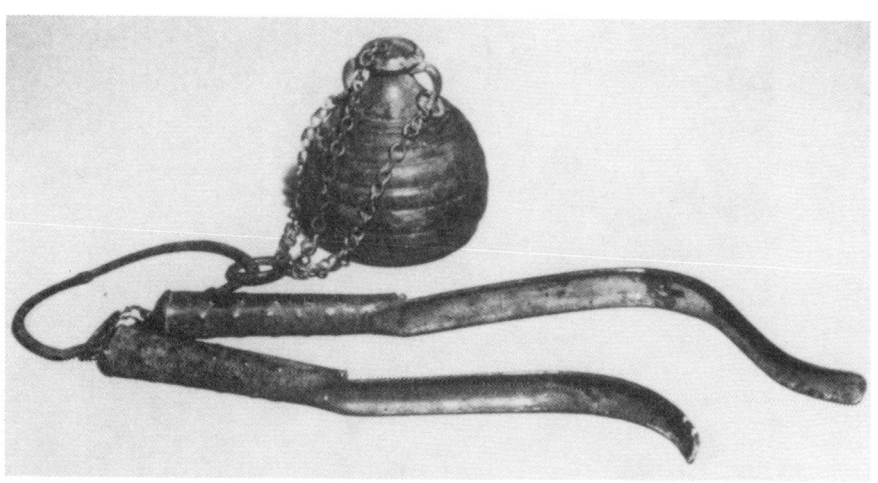

Fig. 6 Strigils, or scrapers, and oil vase used by athletes.

These symbols identify Aurelius as a boxer. There is also strong evidence that he was a wrestler and pancratiast (a competition combining both wrestling and boxing). The same athlete in antiquity usually competed in all three events, referred to as the "heavy sports."

The oil vase, strigils, and gloves were the personal implements used by Aurelius in his athletic career. Athletes rubbed olive oil on their skin before exercising, to keep dirt out of their pours and to prevent sunburn. The oil was kept in a small vase called an *aryballos*. Before competition the athletes dusted themselves with a coat of fine sand to help the offensive athlete get a firm grip on his otherwise slippery opponent. While the intention behind the use of oil and sand was to help the competitor on the offense, a well known ploy of the ancient palaestra was to apply a superabundance of oil on the neck and shoulders, hindering the opponent's ability to throw his slippery adversary! After the competition, the sand was removed from the body with a scraper called a strigil (Fig. 6). In ancient Greece wrestlers were often buried with their strigils.

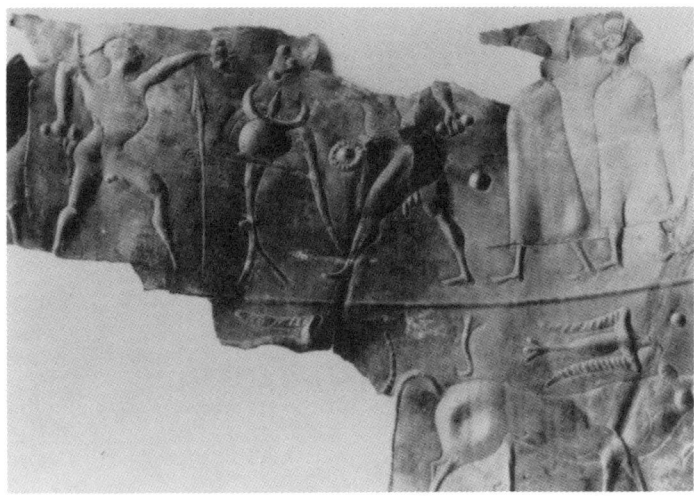

Fig. 7   Illyrian bronze engraving of boxers.

The boxing gloves were the final characteristic piece of athletic equipment on the marker. When first observed, these figures were thought to be dumbbells, but other archaeological evidence clearly identifies the objects as a type of boxing glove (Fig. 7). The boxer gripped the middle of these leather-covered, weighted objects and then fastened them to his wrists with straps. Thus they were not "gloves" in the accepted sense. They were weapons designed to hurt, rather than to protect an opponent in a bout. The edges of the gloves were used to lacerate the defender's face. Bouts continued until one of the competitors either quit, was knocked unconscious, or was killed.

While the three oval symbols on the Helix stone (Fig. 3) have been described by some as victory urns and prize-money purses, they were probably agonistic crowns.[26] Similar symbols appear on a number of coins from Asia Minor (Figs. 8 and 9), on a painted vase and on a Lydian sarcophagus. An interesting Hierapolitan coin depicts a young man with a palm in one hand while with the other he supports a crown on his head.[27] The crowning of victorious athletes occurs frequently in classical literature. Inscribed crowns had the name of the festival they commemorated. The crowns on Aurelius's epitaph, however, were inscribed with the name of the city which sponsored the various festivals that he won (as distinguished from the festivals' names). Two of the cities on Helix's crowns (Sebaste and Stektorion) were within a day's journey from Eumeneia, while the third city (Brundisium) was in Italy.

Athletes and gladiators were frequently granted honorary citizenship by the cities sponsoring the festivals at which they were victorious. Champions often accumulated multiple citizenships. These were the "other cities" of which Aurelius said he was a citizen in addition to Eumeneia. Helix was more than simply an athletic competitor -- he was a champion.

Figs. 8 and 9   Agonistic crowns shown on coins from Asia Minor.

Aurelius Helix chose an interesting word in Greek to refer to his tomb. The word he used was *heroon*. This was a pagan term filled with pagan religious ideas. The Greeks venerated the remains of dead "heroes" (derived from *heroon*) and a cultic and civic significance was attached to their grave sites.[28] The medieval cult of the saints grew out of this pagan hero worship. Aurelius Helix called his tomb literally "the resting place of a hero," which in itself is filled with a hidden wealth of meaning.

The early church had mixed attitudes toward ancient sports because the festivals were steeped in pagan myth and ritual. Ironically, many prominent Christians used athletic imagery as a metaphor for the conflict between Christian and pagan culture. Christians adopted a change in attitude toward pagan athletics which was influenced by changed attitudes within Hellenistic Judaism.[29] This change is reflected in the New Testament, which is filled with athletic terminology. Biblical writers used agonistic terminology to teach ethical concepts to pagan converts. Perhaps Aurelius found a justification for his athletic career in the Apostle Paul's references to boxing and wrestling in the New Testament.[30]

There are numerous classical and early Christian references to the morally redeeming virtue of athletic competition.[31] An intriguing point was made by the pagan orator Dio Chrysostom (A.D. 30-112) in his *Orations*. He referred to a boxer named Melankomas, renowned for his superior strength, self-control and moderation. Melankomas won all of his bouts without having to fight aggressively.[32] He would simply keep his adversary at bay with an extended arm until his opponent became exhausted, futilely attempting to land punches. For Dio Chrysostom and many others in antiquity, Melankomas exemplified true virtue. He overcame adversity with self-restraint. It is intriguing to think about how Helix might have viewed himself against a popular tradition like that of Melankomas. As a Christian, Helix was exhorted to strive for virtue in his life, yet in his leisure, he pummeled pagan opponents in the Greek games.

A strong opposition arose in the church to condemn athletics. Tertullian, living in the shadow of the Carthaginian colosseum, forcefully renounced the Roman festivals. In the *Apologeticum*, he reasoned,

> We renounce your public games as much as we do their origins, which we know to stem from superstition . . . we have nothing to do in speech, sight, or sound with the insanity of the circus, the shamelessness of the theater, the heinousness of the arena, the vanity of physical education.[33]

In *De spectaculis* Tertullian passionately condemned the circus, gladiatorial combat, the amphitheater, and all athletic contests. He warned Christian catechumens not to attend the public spectacles. The Roman games were sinful because of their pagan origins and because they excited uncontrollable passion in the spectator, which was inharmonious with the Christian religion.

> Now if you insist that the stadium is mentioned in Scripture, you will win that point. But you will not deny that what is done in the stadium is unworthy of your sight, blows of the fists, kicks, poundings, every assault of the hand and attack upon man's face, which is the image of God. You will never approve of silly racing and hurling and even sillier jumping, never will empty and ingenious displays of power please you, nor the attention paid to an artificially developed body as it has gone beyond God's proper craft; and you will hate the men fed full on account of Greek pastimes. Wrestling is also the Devil's work: the Devil crushed men first. Its attack is the serpent's power, clinging to hold, twisting to bind, slippery for escape.[34]

It should be noted that Tertullian was an outspoken puritan. Later in his life (around A.D. 207), Tertullian joined the Montanist sect. Both of the works quoted above were probably written by Tertullian before his conversion to Montanism. However, many of his works written prior to A.D. 207 contain strong anti-Roman and rigoristic sentiments that are closely associated with the Montanists. It is noteworthy that Aurelius lived, half a century later, in the midst of the Montanists, who certainly must have held a position opposed to athletics similar to that of Tertullian.

Another Christian puritanical rigorist who lived in the third century A.D. and addressed the issue of pagan sports was Novatian. In the tract *De spectaculis* Novatian explicitly condemned Christians who would even watch pagan sporting events.

> Among the faithful and those who lay claim to the dignity of a Christian calling, some find no shame, no shame, I say--in vindicating from the heavenly Scriptures, the vain superstitions of the pagans that are intermingled in the spectacles . . . "Where," they ask, "are such things mentioned in Scripture? Where are they prohibited? . . . A struggling apostle paints for us the picture of a boxing match and of our own wrestling against the spiritual forces of wickedness . . . Why then should a faithful Christian not be at liberty to be a spectator of things that the divine Writings are at liberty to mention." I can with reason state here that it would have been far better for such people to lack knowledge of the Scriptures than to read them in such a manner![35]

The church historians reserved agonistic epithets for martyrs. They referred to the martyrs as holy wrestlers and God's noble athletes triumphing for piety in the arena of persecution.[36] This should be contrasted with Helix, who lived during the Decian persecution and dedicated a courageous epitaph, but who wrestled for temporal praise. By the fourth century the church formally barred athletes and spectators from baptism, adopting the standard first referred to by Tertullian in *De spectaculis*.[37]

Aurelius Eutychus also shared in the municipal life of Eumeneia. By virtue of his citizenship, he was a member of the city council. But Helix was given the higher distinction of being elected to the Board of Elders (*Geraios*). Like his participation in sports, his infiltration into the local political administration is filled with pagan implications. The local governments were often responsible for the prosecution and punishment of Christians.

Instead of viewing Helix as a compromiser with idolatry, we may see his motives and goals as noble. According to Eusebius, there was a town in Phrygia that was entirely Christian.[38] Several other Christian epitaphs at Eumeneia boast that the deceased were members of the local political council.[39] Aurelius and his Christian colleagues may have served in the local government to protect the other Christians in Eumeneia.

There were several negative attitudes, however, maintained by the early church toward Christian political activism. Tertullian vehemently argued that Christians should disassociate themselves from civic responsibilities and flee from the idolatry associated with the Roman government.[40] Church fathers like Clement of Alexandria (circa A.D. 150-220), reasoned that the church should remain apolitical.[41] And Origen (circa A.D. 185-254) believed that the Christian held a heavenly citizenship and should be dedicated to bringing the Kingdom of God to earth.[42]

The syncretism in Aurelius Eutychus's epitaph is astounding. Whether he was born a Christian, or if not, whether his pagan exploits preceded his conversion to Christianity, is immaterial. Both the Christian and pagan elements were engraved for all to see. The gravestone is an extraordinary witness not only to an individual's social and athletic achievements but also to his personal faith in the midst of state crisis and church debate. Helix's gravestone dedication, like all such, was a monument to his own ego. The epitaph and carvings on his stone secure an opportunity for one like Aurelius Eutychus, also called Helix, who would otherwise be forgotten, to be remembered, and to a degree, to become immortal.

NOTES

This article is dedicated with gratitude to the author's mentor, Dr. Edwin Yamauchi, Professor of Ancient History at Miami University and an avid scholar and sports fan. The author is grateful to Mason Hammond, Pope Professor of Latin Language and Literature, *Emeritus*, at Harvard University, for reviewing the manuscript and making helpful editorial suggestions. The photographs in Figures 2, 3 and 4 are reproduced by courtesy of *The Journal of Roman Studies*, in Figure 5 of Soprintendenza alle Antichita di Ostia (B699), in Figure 6 of the British Museum (B2455), in Figure 7 of the Tiroler Landesmuseum Ferdinandeum (ins. 2274), in Figure 8 of the Libraire d'Amérique et d'Orient Hellenica XI, pl. 34 no. 10, and in Figure 9 of the British Museum Department of Coins and Medals (coin of Phrygia, Synnada 28).

1. See R. Lattimore, *Themes in Greek and Latin Epitaphs* (Urbana: University of Illinois Press, 1962); Louis Robert, *Die Epigraphik der klassischen Welt* (Bonn: Rudolph Habelt Verlag, 1970); and G. Susini, *The Roman Stonecutter* trans. by A.M. Dabrowski, ed. with intr. by E. Badian (Oxford: Blackwell, 1973).

2. For primary sources consult W. Dittenberger, ed., *Orientis Graeci Inscriptiones Selectae* 2 Vols. (repr. New York: Olms, 1970); J. Keil, et al, eds., *Monumenta Asiae Minoris Antiqua* 9 Vols. (Manchester: University Press, 1928-) ; D. LeBas and W.H. Waddington, ed., *Inscription Grècques et Latines* (Paris: E. Leroux, 1870); and D. LeBas and W.H. Waddington, ed., *Voyage archéologique en Grèce et en Asie Mineure* 3 Vols. (Paris: Firmin-Didot Frères, Fils et Cie, 1847-77). See also for surveys and primary sources C.H.E. Haspels, *The Highlands of Phrygia* (Princeton: Princeton University Press, 1971); W.M. Ramsay, *The Cities and Bishoprics of Phrygia* 2 Vols. (Oxford: Oxford University Press, 1895-97; repr. New York: Arno Press, 1976); and Louis Robert, *Études anatoliennes; récherches sur les inscriptions grècques de l'Asie Mineure* (Paris: E. de Boccard,1937).

3. W.M. Calder in his "Philadelphia and Montanism," *Bulletin of the John Rylands Library* 7 (1922-23): 310 n.1, 317, has noted that the Roman catacombs should not be compared with epitaphs because the catacombs were not dedicated openly for all to see.

4. For a thorough treatment and bibliography see Elsa Gibson, The "Christians for Christians" Inscriptions of Phrygia, *Harvard Theological Studies*, Vol. 32 (Missoula, Mont.: Scholars Press, 1978).

5. See Ramsay, *Cities* (note 2), 491; J.G.C. Anderson, "Paganism and Christianity in the Upper Tembris Valley," *Studies in the History and Art of the Eastern Roman Provinces*. Aberdeen University Studies 20 (Aberdeen: University Press, 1906), 201; Calder, "Philadelphia and Montanism" (note 3); Idem., "Epigraphy of Anatolian Heresies," *Anatolian Studies Presented to Sir William Ramsay* (Manchester: University Press,

1923); Idem., "Leaves from an Anatolian Notebook," *Bulletin of the John Rylands Library* 13 (1929), 254-71; Idem., "Early Christian Epitaphs From Phrygia," *Anatolian Studies* 5 (1955), 25-38; H. Grègoire, "Épigraphie chrètienne (Les inscriptions heretiques d'Asie Mineure)," *Byzantion* 1 (1924), 695-710; and C. Cecchelli, *Monumenti cristiano-eretici di Roma* (Rome: Palombi, 1944), 84. On the Montanists, see N. Bonwetsch, *Texte zur Geschichte des Montanismus* KIT 129 (Bonn: Marcus, 1914); P. de Labriolle, *La crise Montaniste* (Paris: Leroux, 1913); Idem., *Les sources de l'histoire du Montanisme* (Paris: Leroux, 1913); and W. Schepelern, *Der Montanismus und die Phrygiscen Kulte*, trans. by W. Baur (Tubingen: J.C.B. Mohr/Paul Siebeck, 1929).

6. See Gibson, *"Christians for Christians"* (note 4); P. de Labriolle, *La crise* (note 5), 489; Schepelern, *Der Montanismus* (note 5), 80-2; A. Ferrua, "Questioni di epigrafia eretica romana," *RivArchCrist* 21 (1945), 218-21 and Idem., "Di una comunita Montanista sull Aurelia alla fine del IV secolo," *CivCatt* 87 (1936), 2.216-27; and H. Gregoire et al., *Les Persecutions dans l'Empire Romain*, Mémoires de l'Académie royale de Belgique, Classe des lettres et des sciences morales et politiques, 2nd series, 46,1 (1951), 18.

7. Gibson, *"Christians for Christians"* (note 4), 144. See also Susini, *Stonecutter* (note 1), 47-8.

8. W.M. Calder, "The Eumeneian Formula," *Anatolian Studies Presented to William Hepworth Buckler* (Manchester: University Press, 1939).

9. Lattimore, *Themes* (note 1), 106-25.

10. See Calder, "Leaves" (note 5), 255-60; and W.H. Buckler et al., "III.- Monuments From Central Phrygia," *JRS* 16 (1926), 80-2; no. 204; L. Robert, *Hellenica* XI-XII, 423-5.

11. The inscription was first published by P. Paris, "Inscriptions D'Eumenia," *B.C.H.* 7 (1884), 234 no. 2; and by Ramsay, *Cities* (note 2), 522.

12. Calder, "Leaves" (note 5), 257.

13. Calder, "Philadelphia" (note 3), 318, 345.

14. Ramsay, *JHS* (1883), 30.

15. The Emperors, like the Greek gods, were shown honor by athletic contests. An imperial temple was situated in Aurelius Eutychus's town of Eumeneia. For further details see S.R.F. Price, *Rituals and Power: The Roman Imperial Cult in Asia Minor* (London: Cambridge University Press, 1984).

16. cf. Acts 20.9.

17. Ramsay, *Cities* (note 2), 522. See Rom. 16.14 and the Apostolic work entitled the *Shepherd of Hermas*; also note 2 Tim. 1.15. There is a remote possibility that the name Hermes refers to the Greek god instead of an actual person. Hermes was the patron god of wrestlers. Helix might be boasting that his natural "god-given" athletic abilities associate him with Hermes.

18. See Th. Nissen, *Vita S. Abercii* (Leipzig: B.G. Teubner, 1910); and W.M. Calder, "The Epitaph of Aviricius Marcellus," *JRS* 29 (1939): 1-4; and Ramsay, *Cities* (note 2), 709-33.

19. In classical antiquity many people belonged to burial societies organized around trade guilds. These societies took care of the details of interment for their members, including at times the dedication of the decedent's epitaph. Some of the most intriguing dedications were made by gladiators in honor of a fallen colleague.

20. See the article by Eve D'Ambra entitled "A Myth for a Smith: A Meleager Sarcophagus from a Tomb in Ostia," *American Journal of Archaeology* 92, 1 (1988), 85-99.

21. B.V. Head, *Catalogue of the Greek Coins in the British Museum* Phrygia; ed. by R.S. Poole (London: British Museum, 1906; repr. Bologna: A. Forni, 1981), pl. 48 no. 4.

22. See description by Ramsay in *JHS* 25 (1905), 174 no. 56.

23. Buckler et al., "III. - Monuments" (note 10), 85 no. 210.

24. D'Ambra, "A Myth for a Smith" (note 20), 99.

25. Lucian, *Dial. meretr.* 6.

26. Buckler et al., "Monuments" (note 10), 81.

27. F. Imhoof-Blumer, "Coin-Types of Some Kilikian Cities," *Journal of Hellenic Studies* 18 (1898), 179 no. 52 Pl. XIII no. 18.

28. Ramsay, *Cities* (note 2), 517-8; and Lattimore, *Themes* (note 1), 97, 316.

29. See M. Hengel, *Judaism and Hellenism* (Philadelphia: Fortress Press, 1975); A. Harris, *Greek Athletics and the Jews* (Cardiff, 1976); R.R. Chambers, "Greek Athletics and the Jews 165 B.C. - A.D. 70," Dissertation, Miami University, 1980; and M. Poliakoff, "Jacob, Job, and Other Wrestlers: Reception of Greek Athletics by Jews and Christians in Antiquity," *Journal of Sport History* 11, 2 (1984), 48-65.

30. 1 Cor. 9.24-7. See Poliakoff, "Jacob, Job, and Other Wrestlers" (note 29), 54; and V. Pfitzner, *Paul and the Agon Motif* (Leiden: Brill, 1962).

Scott T. Carroll

31. R. Merkelbach, "Der Griechische Wortschatz und die Christen," *Zeitschr. für Papyrol. und Epigraph.* 18 (1975): 101-48; and A. Koch, "Leibesübungen im Frühchristentum und in der Beginnenden Volkwanderungszeit," *Geschichte der Leibesübungen* 2 (Berlin -Munich-Frankfurt, 1972), 312-40.

32. Dio Chrysostom, *Orations* 29.14; and L. Robert, *Hellenica* 11-12 (Paris, 1960), 338-9.

33. Tertullian, *Apology* 38.

34. Tertullian, *De spectaculis* 18.

35. Novatian, *De spectaculis* 2.

36. Note R.L. Fox, *Pagans and Christians* (New York: Alfred A. Knopf, Inc., 1987), 436, 439, 442. See Eusebius, *Hist. eccl.* 8.7-8; Idem., *Acta martyr.* 3.

37. *Apostolic Constitution* 8.32.

38. Eusebius, *Hist. eccl.* 8.11.

39. A.R.R. Sheppard, "Jews, Christians and Heretics in Acmonia and Eumeneia," *Anatolian Studies* 29 (1979), 170-1, 180.

40. Tertullian, *De Idololatria* 11.4, 17-18.

41. Clement of Alexandria, *Stromateis* 5.14.98.

42. Origen, *Contra Celsum* 3.30, 8.75.

Fig. 126 Exercise Conant, 1722, Mansfield Center

The Colonial Burying Grounds of Eastern Connecticut and The Men Who Made Them, by James A. Slater. Photographs by Daniel and Jessie Lie Farber. Hamden, CT: Published for the Connecticut Academy of Arts and Sciences by Archon Books, 1987. Price: $65.

Review by Peter Benes

James A. Slater's long-awaited publication on eastern Connecticut gravestones 1687-1820 represents the culmination of years of patient fieldwork and study by a uniquely qualified scholar. An entomologist in the Department of Ecology and Evolutionary Biology of the University of Connecticut at Storrs, the author has enlarged upon his own avocational research on this subject with the published and unpublished notes and papers of the late Ernest Caulfield, M.D. He has applied to his study systematic data gathering procedures which took him to scores of obscure and hard-to-find burying sites in the study region. The result is a thoroughly researched and readable work of major importance in the field which fulfills the promise shown in the author's three earlier publications on individual carvers: one undertaken in collaboration with Dr. Caulfield on the Lebanon (Connecticut) stonecarver Obadiah Wheeler (1972); the second undertaken with Ralph Tucker on the Essex County (Massachusetts) and Norwich (Connecticut) carver John Hartshorne; and the third on the Coventry (Connecticut) carvers Jonathan and John Loomis. All of these publications follow a somewhat similar research method, and all are documented by the superb photographs of Daniel and Jessie Lie Farber.

In keeping with its title, Slater's newest and most ambitious study is divided into two parts. The first concerns the identification of seventy-five named or hypothesized carvers who placed stones in Eastern Connecticut during the period. An accompanying commentary explores the source and evolution of each carver's style; a stone distribution table designating specific sites summarizes the range and geographical density of each carver's work. The second offers a practical guide to 201 colonial period burying grounds in fifty-nine eastern Connecticut towns and includes directions for locating every site. A capsule history of each community is followed by an informal commentary on some of the more interesting and representative markers found at the site. Tables quantitatively summarize the work of carvers represented in each community. Each section is extensively illustrated with maps, line drawings, and photographs and occasional rubbings of sample stone styles. The illustrations are well selected and offer pleasant surprises: the poignant Dewey children stone (possibly by Lebbeus Kimball), and the Joseph and Judith Laevens stone by Jonathan Roberts are among the many that appear for the first time in print. A varied assortment of close-up details, whole stones, and views of burying sites provides an appropriate visual balance. A complete index, definition of terms, and introductory essay on geology and style complete the book.

The reader of this volume is amply rewarded by Slater's patience. Characterized by a regional or naive aesthetic, the gravestone trade in eastern Connecticut flourished on the peripheries of commercial and academic stonecarving traditions emanating from the Connecticut River Valley, from the urban Rhode Island and the Narragansett area, and from Boston. The numerous variations on indigenous styles, and the continuing evolutionary thread of these styles in a milieu intermingling with outside styles and stone sources provide the chief substance and intellectual strength of the volume. It is here that the author's experience with fine differences in insect morphology leads the reader to appreciate and understand subtle differences in carver styles where most students, this reviewer included, previously saw only similarities. Slater's sensitivity and his empirical caution are reflected in the names he gives to unidentified carvers: "The False Huntington Carver," "The Chaplin-Helmet-Manning Imitator," "The Drake Imitator."

Readers should not be misled by Dr. Slater's (refreshingly) unassuming writing style or by his "handbook" approach to a subject that in recent years has been characterized by impressionistic, art-historical analysis. The field work necessary to collect the material is formidable and would have daunted anyone else except, perhaps, a professional biologist trained in gathering and analyzing large quantities of minute data. The stone distribution tables are based on approximately 20,000 extant markers, each of which was examined, recorded and classified by the author. The Manning family stones alone number 2,422. In the field of decorative arts scholarship and material culture studies, a data base of this magnitude is unprecedented and constitutes a groundbreaking and innovative use of quantitative analysis--made possible, of course, by the immobility and relatively high rate of survival of grave markers in the greater world of antique objects. In the specific field of gravestone scholarship, it applies the methodology of stone distribution analysis to a wider geographic scope than has been hitherto attempted. The tables provide the single most valuable data of this type to appear in print to date and allow the reader to perceive unassisted the complex genealogical, commercial, social, and cultural processes that these distribution patterns suggest.

Like all good studies, *The Colonial Burying Grounds of Eastern Connecticut* raises as many new questions as it answers old ones. Not attempted in this work is any systematic explanation of the distribution of stones, especially the "outlier" stones such as the Boston-area slates found in Woodstock, a town located in the northeast sector of the state. By pointing out that Woodstock was founded by former residents of Roxbury, Massachusetts, Slater demonstrates he has a keen and sensitive understanding of such patterns. But numerous questions remain. Why, for example, does a gravestone carved by Jonas Stewart appear in East Lyme, Connecticut, ninety miles from its point of origin in Charlestown, New Hampshire? The reverse question is also unanswered: why should the gravestones of "The Hampton Indian" be almost wholly restricted to two eastern Connecticut parishes while Peter Barker's stones -- certainly as naive and technically incompetent as those of the "The Hampton Indian" -- be spread over a wide range of southern coastal Connecticut? Dr. Slater suggests quietly that Barker was an itinerant; and, indeed, this stonecutter evidently was. Determining the explanation for all of these "outlier" stones would be a fascinating but monumental task. But in his self-discipline and cautious use of data, the reader may suspect Dr. Slater modestly kept some of the answers to himself.

A larger unanswered question raised by Slater's study concerns cultural practices within eastern Connecticut itself. Why did a relatively small group of New England interior rural communities patronize stonecarvers who followed a succession of simplistic, inventive, energetic, naive--and at times outrageous--designs? Were the communities themselves naive, energetic, and inventive? Slater cautiously refers to eastern Connecticut as "the core areas of indigenous gravestone carving in North America" (p. xviii). But he does not address the question whether eastern Connecticut was a relict cultural zone. Were there parallel characteristics in the folk speech of eastern Connecticut? In farmyard architecture? Field patterns and fencing styles? Hairstyles and dress? This brings to mind Sarah Kemble Knight's observation in 1704 that Connecticut women were "very plain" in their dress, but "follow one another in their modes [so closely]..that You may know where they belong...meet them where you will." When the Englishman William Strickland toured the northeastern United States in 1794 and 1795, he reported finding West-of-England speech characteristics and agricultural practices in Coventry, Connecticut, among the latter the practice of irrigating fields from water that ran off public roads. This also brings to mind the unusual cluster of orange meeting houses in the northeast Connecticut towns of Pomfret, Brooklyn, Killingly, and Hampton during and just following the years that the Mannings and their imitators left stones in these communities. Do gravestones offer any insight into other ingrown or indigenous cultural practices in eastern Connecticut? Again, to answer these questions would involve far more research and a much larger book. Perhaps the real contribution of Slater's work still lies at some future point in time when enough is known of eastern Connecticut speech characteristics, dress styles, or decorative arts practices of the colonial period to allow a side-by-side comparison of two or more vernacular practices from a specific region.

The book is not without weaknesses. The price will regrettably keep this important imprint out of the private libraries of many deserving readers. Copy editing is uneven and is reflected most conspicuously in the book's title: the men who "made" the colonial burying grounds of Eastern Connecticut are the sextons who dug graves, carpenters who erected fences, and the town committees that set aside and surveyed burying plots. The men who made Connecticut *gravestones* were the stone carvers that Slater writes about. The spellings "esthetic" and "aesthetic" occur on the same page (p. xvi). The subheadings of part one are out of sequence with those provided in the summary listing on pages 3 and 4. Desperately needed is an index or list of carvers, including unidentified carvers and a crossfile on the different colloquial names given to unidentified carvers by Caulfield, by Slater, and by other field-workers. Desperately needed, too, are summary lists or section headings under each chapter in the table of contents. These organizational aids could have replaced the redundant list of illustrations on pages viii-xiv.

The reader will find what amounts to two entirely different organizational modes in Slater's study and must be prepared to find two books. The carver-identification section is arranged by geological sub-region:

granite carvers, sandstone carvers, eastern Massachusetts slate carvers, northeast sector local carvers, and extra-limital carvers. The order followed by Slater within sub-regions lists earlier or more important carvers sometimes before later or less important ones; the resulting sequence retains a cohesive geographic/geological order that generally leads the reader east to west or south to north. The burying ground section, however, is arranged alphabetically by the name of early town limits and thus seems to "wander" without direction. In the best of possible worlds, Dr. Slater might have arranged both sections to "drift" in the same direction, thus providing a unifying parallel. The alphabetical arrangement of towns in the second part might have been segregated into the same geologically defined sub-regional groupings as part one--the initial group of alphabetically listed towns would be those where granite stones are predominantly found; the second group of alphabetically arranged towns, where sandstone markers are predominantly found, and so on. It must be recognized, on the other hand, that many of the stones are not indigenous to the areas where they are found: Connecticut Valley stones were carried in large numbers down the river into the Sound and set up in New London, East Lyme and other towns; the Newport, Rhode Island, school of carvers is richly represented in these burying grounds; and as one moves northward in the Connecticut Valley the influence of Longmeadow and Springfield carvers becomes greater and greater. Accordingly, an arrangement different from that selected by Dr. Slater might well prove impractical.

Slater's study of early Connecticut grave markers is appropriately dedicated to the two students who did more than any other individuals to pioneer gravestone scholarship in New England, Harriette M. Forbes and Ernest Caulfield. Mrs. Forbes published her gravestone work in 1927; however, Dr. Caulfield's study was terminated by his progressive blindness before he could assemble and organize his materials into a coherent body.

Book Review

Even though a number of Caulfield's articles on individual carvers appeared posthumously in the *Connecticut Historical Society Bulletin*, the loss to scholarship was a major one. By bringing into the public domain much of the unpublished original research that still remained in Dr. Caulfield's papers, the present volume does much to offset this loss and is as much a testament to Dr. Slater's compassionate mastery of his subject as it is to his generous and enlightened spirit.

Fig. 163   Dorothy Sluman, 1754, Old Tollard.

Fig. 96　Mary Torrey, 1792, Old Brooklyn Burying Ground.

Contributors

Peter Benes is the founder of The Dublin Seminar for New England Folklife and editor of its annual proceedings, a founder of the Association for Gravestone Studies and author of many articles on gravestones and stonecutters. His best known work is *The Masks of Orthodoxy*.

Scott T. Carroll obtained his Master of Arts degree at Trinity College and became a candidate for a Ph.D. at Miami University in Ohio. He is now an Assistant Professor of Ancient History and Languages at Gordon College, Wenham, Massachusetts. He is interested in a variety of areas including ancient religion, sports and languages and is currently studying Coptic tombstones between the fourth and eighth centuries, A.D.

Paula J. Fenza holds a Masters degree in Anthropology from Northern Illinois University and is a doctoral candidate at the University of Chicago. She has written a number of articles on history and archaeology for the Kendall County Bicentennial Commission. Her interest in cemeteries was inspired by her mother, an avid enthusiast of the subject.

Angelika Krüger-Kahloula attended the Universities of Frankfurt, Bristol, Toronto and Orleans and received her doctorate from the J.W. Goethe-Universität in Frankfurt. She has taught in the American Studies departments of the Universities of Munich and Frankfurt and was a fellow at the Afro-American Studies Department of Yale in 1985-1986 when most of the research for her paper was done. She currently teaches English, French and Spanish at the senior high school level in West Germany.

M. Ruth Little has a Master of Arts degree in Art History from Brown University and a Ph.D. in Art History and Folklore from the University of North Carolina. She conducted the North Carolina Gravemarker Survey with a grant from the National Endowment for the Humanities in 1980-1982. She is currently National Register Coordinator for the North Carolina State Historic Preservation Office and is working on a book based on this survey.

Nancy-Lou Patterson is a Professor of Fine Arts at the University of Waterloo in Waterloo, Ontario.

Laura Sue Sanborn holds two degrees from the University of Michigan and is an Assistant Professor of Landscape Architecture and Environmental Planning at Utah State University, where she has taught since 1983.

Eloise Sibley West has a Masters degree in Clinical and Abnormal Psychology from Ohio State University. She lives in Fitchburg, Massachusetts, has been an active member of the Association for Gravestone Studies since its founding and has served several terms as a trustee.

Index of Carvers, and of Illustrated Gravestones and their Location

Albuquerque, 161, 169, 174
Allenford United Church, Allenford, Bruce County, 188, 189
Anatolia, 211
Armstrong, Elizabeth, 199
Ashby, 10
Attleboro, 66

Bailey, Susanah, 23
Ball, Lieut. Jeremiah, 16
Barker, Peter, 236
Barkin, Ernest L., 118
Bieth, Caroline, 180
Brainerd, Silas, 72, 80
Brown, John Dwight, 19
Brown, Joseph, 19
Buncombe Baptist Churchyard, Petersville, 125
Burnham, Daniel family graves, 142

Caesar, 66
Chilcher family, 143
China Grove Baptist Churchyard, Cumberland County, 123
Clap, David, 13
Coachman, William Randolph, 130
Conant, Exercise, 232
Cowden, Thomas, 17
Culbreth, Renial, 102, 111, 112, 113, 114, 115, 119
Cumings, Lt. Archelaus, 22

Dolph, John, 28
Dorchester, 7, 10, 12, 13
Dwight, daughter of John and Susanna, 14
Dwight, Francis, 1, 4, 18, 19, 20, 21, 22, 24, 25, 29
Dwight, John, 1, 26
Dwight, Sullivan, 18, 22, 25

Edmondson, William, 133
Elmwood Cemetery, 149
Erin Cemetery, Erin, Wellington County, 187
Espanola, 158
Eutychus, Aurelius, 214, 215

First Baptist Church, Sampson County, 112
Fitchburg, 6, 17
Flea Hill Church, Cumberland County, 118
Flemington Community Cemetery, New Hanover County, 122
Flova, 58
Forest Home Cemetery, 143, 150, 151
Foster, Ruth, 10

Gainey, Frances G., 110
Galisteo, 168
Gaschet, Levi, 11
Geddie, John and Laura, 115
Grace United Church, Millbank, Waterloo County, 201
Graceland Cemetery, 136, 141, 142, 153
Graves family, 141
Groton, 8, 15

Hampton Indian, The, 236
Hank's Chapel AME Churchyard, New Hanover County, 128
Hartshorne, John, 233
Harvard, 32, 41
Hill Graveyard, Wilmington, New Hanover County, 128
Hoffman, Johannes, 204
How, Deacon Josiah, 17

Isham, John, 80

Jaffrey Center, 23

Kelly-McLaurin Graveyard, Cumberland County, 115
Kimball, Lebbeus, 234
Kruesinca, Agnes, 154

Little, James F., 128
Locke, James, 10
Loomis, John, 233
Loomis, Jonathan, 233
Lunenberg, 8

Manning, Josiah, 87, 100
Mansfield Center, 232
Martin, Willie S., 201
McAlister, Jannie J., 120
McEachin, Issiah, 111, 116, 117, 118, 119
McGoogan, Jane, 145
McLaurin, Irene, 102
McLaurin, Dixon, 113
McLellan, Peter and Catherine, 190
McNaughton, Henry, 187
Melvin, O.A., 123
Metchel, Martha, 8
Miller, Alexander, 198
Milton, 17
Morton, Capt. Edmund, 12
Mt. Zion AMEZ Churchyard, Cumberland County, 102, 110, 113

Northern New Hanover County, 131

Old Brooklyn Burying Ground, 240
Old Smith Grove Baptist Churchyard, Davidson County, 126
Old Tollard, 239
Othello, 32, 41
Owens, Clinnie M., 112

Paddock, Harold "Buddy", 146
Palmer, Potter family, 136
Park family, 13, 14
Patterson, William L., 151
Peralta, 161, 162, 164, 165, 167, 175
Pierce, Patty, 6
Preston Cemetery, Cambridge, Waterloo County, 180
Princeton, 58, 59
Proctor, William, 189

Resurrection Cemetery, Justice, 145
Ritzma, Annie, 154
Roberts, Jonathan, 234
Rockwood, Lieut. Elisha, 15
Rushes Cemetery, Waterloo County, 199

Sawtell, David, 24, 25
Sawtell, Lieut. Hezekiah, 8
Shirley, vi, 14, 26
Show Hill AME Zion Churchyard, Cumberland County, 120
Simonds, William, vi
Sluman, Dorothy, 239
Spears, Flora, 122
St. Andrew's Presbyterian Church Cemetery, Perth County, 190
St. Boniface Roman Catholic Church, Maryhill, 198
St. Peter's Lutheran Cemetery, Neustadt, 194
Stevens, Pompe, 90
Stewart, Jonas, 236
Sullivan, Louis, 139
Swans Creek Baptist Churchyard, Cumberland County, 130

Tecolote, 171
Temple, 22
Thomas, 59
Torrey, Mary, 240
Townsend, 11, 16
Truchas, 177

Verdell, Emma, 125

Wagner, Anna, 194
Walden, John II, 100
Webster, Stephen, 28
Webster, Timothy, 153
Wheeler, Capt. Abraham, 7
Wheeler, Obadiah, 233
Woodlawn Cemetery, 146

FOR LIBRARY
USE ONLY